Family-Based Services

A Solution-Focused Approach

INSOO KIM BERG

W. W. Norton & Company, Inc.
New York   London

A NORTON PROFESSIONAL BOOK

Printed in the United States of America

Composition by Bytheway Typesetting Services, Inc.
Manufacturing by Haddon Craftsmen, Inc.

Berg, Insoo Kim.
    Family based services : a solution-focused approach / Insoo Kim
Berg.
        p.   cm.
    "A Norton professional book"—P. 11.
    Includes bibliographical references and index.
    ISBN 0-393-70162-X
    1. Family services—United States.   2. Home-based family services-
-United States.   3. Family counseling—United States.   I. Title.
HV699.B47   1994
362.82'8'0973—dc20   93-46043   CIP

W. W. Norton & Company, Inc., 500 Fifth Avenue, New York, NY 10110
W. W. Norton & Company, Ltd., 10 Coptic Street, London WC1A 1PU

2   3   4   5   6   7   8   9   0

To families I have met around the world, who have taught me everything I know about working with them. I am wiser for having met them.

Contents

Foreword

THERE HAS BEEN MUCH interest in how the field of family therapy can be applied to social services in general and child welfare in particular. While the ideas of systems thinking have begun to be used in public and private agencies serving families that have experienced child abuse, child neglect, and delinquency, there has often been a "curious dearth of consistency" between family empowerment thinking and the delivery of services. The emphasis of this book is on the strength, competency, and resiliency that families have to deal with difficulties in their lives. It is sometimes challenging to recognize such qualities in crisis-prone or physically violent families, but Insoo Kim Berg provides not only methods for identifying such resources but suggestions for utilizing these resources to empower families.

Family-Based Services offers ways to apply a solution-focused model of intervention that is effective for such programs as family preservation, home-based family-centered services, family-based services, or any organization aimed at improving services to children and families. I have experienced the benefits of applying this approach with both private and public referrals and have seen an increase in intervention effectiveness and personal satisfaction from using a solution-oriented model.

Practical, respectful, and creative are a few words that describe *Family-Based Services*. Specific ideas are described for working with families who are typically considered the most difficult to treat: families that have not responded to previous treatment, have been identified with "multiple problems," have identified a child as "the problem," are dealing with overwhelming personal and financial hardships, and whose daily experience is one of crisis.

Insoo Kim Berg not only conveys her ideas about working with families in a stimulating manner but communicates a personal respect for families and the difficulties they face. This is reflected in her approach to handling a treatment dilemma such as having to report child abuse while trying to maintain a therapeutic relationship with the family. While recommending concrete ideas, the guiding principle is one of respect for the client's dignity.

Another important element of this book is the uniqueness of every family and every type of solution. Whether the presenting issue is sexual abuse, physical abuse, child neglect, substance abuse, or school problems, the necessity of looking for the exceptional qualities of the individual or family are stressed. This book gives new meaning and new possibilities for those interested in improving their skills in treatment intervention.

John Leverington, Clinical Director
Families, Inc.
West Branch, Iowa

Preface

EVERYBODY KNOWS A LOT about families, since we all grew up in one. Yet the more one knows, the less one seems to know. The family is a wonderful institution that is the source of so much pride and yet so much shame; so strengthening, yet so draining; so nurturing, yet so demanding; so easy to understand, yet so confusing.

Welcome to the exciting, energizing, painful, and exhausting work with families: family-based services (FBS). This work will be the most meaningful and challenging you have ever done and will ever do. It will stretch your mind and help you discover skills and strengths you did not know you had. You will love the work and curse the problems. I assure you that it will be anything but boring.

You will touch the lives of the families you work with in a way that is not possible to measure. The impact you will make on your clients may not be obvious immediately, but they will feel empowered for having traveled a short distance of their lives with you as their guide.

This book is designed to increase your excitement about your work, to ease your pain a little, and to help you to grow through your discovery of the amazing human spirit, both in yourself and in your clients. The clients you will meet in this book will break your heart, touch your soul, and renew your faith in human dignity and spirit, as they did for me.

The idea for this book began while I worked as a consultant-trainer for the protective service unit of a large county social service department. The staff were experienced child welfare workers, some with as many as twenty years of experience in protective service and foster care service. I made home visits for the protective service investigation; I went out with the 24-hour crisis unit whose job was to respond to emergency phone calls in the middle of the night. The cases described here are the clients I treated, supervised, and consulted directly during this period.

Based on 20 years of evolving work at the Brief Family Therapy Center in Milwaukee, Wisconsin, which has been articulated in over 70 articles and numerous books (Berg, 1988; Berg & Miller, 1992; de Shazer, 1982, 1985, 1988, 1991; Dolan, 1991; Kral, 1987; Walter & Peller, 1992), solution-focused therapy is a model that is "simple and elegant," as well as powerful and effective in its application to a variety of presenting problems.

The basic premise of this model is that exceptions to problems offer keys and clues to solving problems and that it is more profitable to pay attention to the activities that center around successful solutions than to the problems. These exceptions become the pathway to future solutions. When and if there are no past successes to build on, the client can be helped to forge a different future by imagining "a miracle" and identifying small but realistically achievable steps toward that event. This is a radically different approach from what is common in the field today.

This book is your guide to this new approach as you wade through mountains of information about the families you work with. It is written in simple language with very little jargon and few technical terms. Following the steps outlined here will take the mystery out of "therapy."

I am grateful to all the families who taught me about their incredible strengths and resiliency in the midst of pain and suffering. My admiration for the supervisors and workers who "fight in the trenches" every day has no limit; they are "the salt of the earth" who deserve more recognition and support from the society that charges them with the awesome responsibility of protecting our future generations.

ACKNOWLEDGMENTS

The writing of this book was a lesson in true collaboration among many gifted and thoughtful people around the world. I have been blessed with family, friends, and colleagues who offered their ideas and suggestions freely and generously. To each one of you I am truly grateful.

I want to thank my husband and colleague, Steve de Shazer, whose boundless patience and support made it possible for me to finish this project. Thanks to my sister, C. J., whose loyal support, friendship, and humor sustain me during difficult times.

A special thank-you to Margaret Farley. Since English is my second language I needed her special help to shape awkward sentences into a readable form. Her gentle prodding and challenges to be clear about what I was really saying were exactly what I needed.

Insoo Kim Berg
Milwaukee, Wisconsin

Family-Based Services

A Solution-Focused Approach

1

What Is Family-Based Services (FBS)?

FAMILY-BASED SERVICES (FBS) is a specialized service in child welfare that focuses on the family as the target of intervention, rather than the child or the parents separately. It adapts the basic knowledge and skills developed in the field of family therapy to thoroughly assess and treat the family as a unit, usually in an intensive, time-limited period.

The philosophical basis of FBS is that the best way to provide services to a child is through strengthening and empowering the family as a unit. Removing the child from the family is traumatic to both the child and the family, no matter what the circumstances of abuse or neglect. Many studies indicate that children placed in alternative care do not fare better over the long run than those children who remained with their parents (Stroul, 1988). Therefore, we believe that strengthening the existing parent-child bond and supporting the parents to do a competent job is the most effective, least intrusive, and most economic way to protect the children in the long run. Clinical experience repeatedly shows that even the badly abused and neglected child longs for his or her own parent and wants to "go home."

FBS is a sensible but drastic shift in the way we think about what is helpful for children and families. It requires specialized knowledge and skills to provide service to the family unit, the parent-child relationship, and other extended family and kinship relationships. FBS is designed to cooperate with the formal and informal network of existing community resources rather than becoming all things to all clients.

By involving the family as a partner in the decision-making and goal-setting process and using the family's existing resources, FBS strives to enhance the family members' sense of control over their own lives. The result is that family members feel an increased sense of competency in conducting their lives and can create a safe and nurturing environment for the children while maintaining the unique cultural and ethnic characteristics of their family unit. With such help, families are able to live independently with a minimum of outside interference.

HOW IS FBS DIFFERENT FROM OTHER SERVICES IN CHILD WELFARE?

For a long time, the field of child welfare took an adversarial position with parents and frequently saw the children as the victims of bad or incompetent parenting. Viewed this way, the solution to a problem was often to separate the children from their parents, putting them in the hands of alternative caretakers, such as foster parents. The intent was to force the parents to learn to be better parents. This period of separation was thought of as a time when the parents learned new and better parenting skills, so that when they were reunited with their children the family would function better.

Parents were told the conditions under which they would be allowed to be reunited with their children, such as getting a job, cleaning up their apartments, learning better parenting skills through attending classes, and engaging in counseling to solve the underlying problems that were thought to cause them to be abusive and neglectful of their children. They were expected to cooperate with social workers and follow their directions. Many parents did just that. Some reluctantly went along with these mandates and successfully reclaimed their children. However, most of these involuntary clients were labeled as "unmotivated" and "resistant to therapy"; it was said that they "minimized their problems" and refused to "own up to their problem."

Furthermore, such practices, based on simple cause and effect notions viewed from an individually oriented perspective, had the effect of creating more hardship and trauma for the children. Not only did the intention of rescuing the children from their bad parents result in punishment for the children, but it also became increasingly difficult to reunite the parents and children the longer they were separated.

Communication was difficult among separate workers assigned to the child, the parent, and the foster parents. When legal issues surfaced, there were cases that had three different attorneys representing three different views of what was good for the family. For example, I once worked with a family of five represented by five different attorneys: one for each parent and one for each of three children because all were above the age of 12 and were entitled to individual legal representation. Instead of encouraging cohesive and cooperative relationships, as was intended, such practices had the effect of fragmenting the family and creating adversarial relationships among the family members.

In recent years, awareness has grown that the best way to help the children is to strengthen the family unit. Several factors have led to this shift in thinking: a renewed recognition of the importance of the emotional bond between children and their parents; the fragmenting effect our child welfare policy has had on the family; the recognition that a lot of money has been spent with very few positive results (Edna McConnell Clark Foundation, 1985), and the recognition that the system simply is not working. Workers' efforts to transform such "involuntary" parents into cooperative, hardworking, and motivated clients able to use individual treatment, support groups, and parenting education classes have had limited success.

Lack of success is often blamed on the hostile and angry personality of the client, his or her lack of education and intelligence, and the impossible demands the system makes on the workers. All these play a part. However, I contend that a more serious problem lies in the way we conceptualize problems and solutions. The goal in child welfare must be to protect children through strengthening their families, not blaming their parents.

For too many years the goal of child welfare has been only the "protection" of children. When the worker's goal is to "protect" a child, it implies that the child needs protection *from* someone, usually the parent. Thus, when a worker enters into a family system uninvited and takes an investigative position on the side of the child against the parent, when the worker tells the parent what she must do, it naturally becomes an adversarial and hostile relationship. To add insult to injury, the parent is often treated as if guilty until proven innocent. It is no wonder that the worker feels frustrated, stressed, and burned out, and that this results in extremely high staff turnover — as high as 50% every six months in some settings.

Let us return to the topic of the clients. These parents are often viewed as having defective and faulty notions of parenting, no problem-solving skills, no interest and ability to become good parents, and lots of psychopathology. Filling such a bottomless pit of deficits and solving "multiproblem" cases is seen as an exhausting and thankless task for the worker.

I believe that it is possible to "treat" mandated cases successfully when the worker sets her sights on clients' strengths rather than on weaknesses, searches for exceptions to the problem, helps construct a different future through "miracle questions," and sets small and achievable goals. The premise of the solution-focused therapy model described here is that change is inevitable, not a hard-won commodity. In following chapters, I will describe the role of the worker, the cornerstone of which is respect and admiration for the client's courage in struggling with the problems of living. This book will describe in detail how to establish a positive client-worker relationship, how to assess for change, how to ask questions that will generate solutions, and various techniques of intervention.

HOW IS FBS COMMONLY PRACTICED?

FBS (also called family preservation, home-based services, or in-home treatment) commonly has the following characteristics:

1. The ultimate purpose is to provide services to the family as a collective unit, with the goal of preserving family unity while insuring the safety of each family member.
2. The delivery of service is intense, immediate, and goal-oriented.
3. Service is provided by a treatment team (often made up of case manager, worker/therapist, and such support staff as the parent educator, homemaker, and so on). Following a period of need assessment, clear treatment goals are set, well-laid-out implementation plans are formulated, and a termination plan is outlined. The client participates in each phase from beginning to end.
4. Each worker carries a limited number of cases for a designated period of time (such as 90 days, 120 days, six months). Most treatment is offered in clients' homes, although some programs offer office visits in combination with the in-home treatment.
5. Some programs combine generic treatment with specialized services for cases involving sexual abuse, alcohol and drug abuse, and domestic violence.
6. FBS is designed to respond to each individual family's unique needs. Therefore, the treatment approach is tailored to fit individual families.
7. Staffing is decided at intake, and frequent case consultation occurs on an ongoing basis.

ADVANTAGES

It is easy to see the advantages of FBS to both clients and workers. Smaller caseloads mean more intense contact with the client family; thus, more information is available to the workers. More frequent observation of the family's functioning gives workers more opportunity to intervene in a timely fashion. With the rapid positive changes clients show, worker enthusiasm is high, clients do better, and cases get closed sooner. The majority of protective cases start out with involuntary clients or clients who are afraid of having their children taken away. They need repeated reassurance not only that the worker is interested in keeping the family together but also that the worker's job is to offer them services that will strengthen family functioning. Clearly, it takes skill and time to influence clients to move beyond their initial reluctance and fear. FBS has had more successes in this respect than traditional child welfare practices.

Working with multiproblem families in any setting can easily overwhelm the worker, who then becomes less effective than he or she could be. By identifying specific, concrete, measurable goals to work toward, sometimes within a limited time, both the client and the worker can mobilize energy and resources, thus increasing the chances of success.

A team approach supports the difficult decisions that workers must continually make. Much of the clinical aspect of child welfare work requires the worker to make judgments and to interpret data that are by their nature ambiguous. Having a team member with another view or a different way of accomplishing the same task increases the options and reassures the worker about safety issues. Having the opinion of another person on your side is simply more reassuring. The experience of many FBS teams across the country has shown that this reduces staff burnout and improves staff morale and enthusiasm for the work. It is not difficult to understand that the energy and excitement the worker feels about what he or she does can easily become contagious — the client can catch it!

DISADVANTAGES

The disadvantages of FBS include the requirement that the worker think differently about her role and conceptualize differently about the families she treats. Instead of being a broker who matches what the client needs with the resources in the community, the worker becomes the treatment person. Thus, FBS requires a new set of skills and new ways of doing things.

FBS requires workers to respond immediately to the needs of the family, to show flexibility and the willingness to do things differently, and to be innovative and creative. It also requires workers to cooperate, become team members, and take risks by exposing their work to colleagues and supervisors.

Most of all, to be successful, FBS requires different organization support and flexibility from management and supervisors, who need to understand and support the FBS philosophy. This is not always easy to accomplish. Without system-wide support, backed by ongoing training and a willingness to reorganize the agency structure if necessary, workers cannot carry out this difficult but rewarding task.

For the worker, it takes time and a shift in the way she approaches her work. She must recognize that the work she does right now may bring about a difference in the client's life sometime in the future. Therefore, the worker must learn to be patient about the client. Time will be required to educate other community systems, such as the schools, courts, medical system, and even other social service agencies, about the unique and creative nature of FBS work.

HOW HAS FBS BEEN INFLUENCED BY FAMILY THERAPY?

The basic concepts and philosophy of family-based services are heavily influenced by family therapy. Family therapy has developed over the past 40 years from a simple observation that an individual's behavior happens within the context of an environment, that the environment influences this behavior, and that, in turn, the environment is influenced by the individual's behavior. Interactionally, since B is part of A's context, what A does influences what B does, and B's reaction influences what A does.

This simple observation expanded the concept of "problem" from being (a) something that an individual has to (b) something that is part of an interactional system. By changing the boundary around the concept of "problem," family therapy also changed the boundary around the parallel concept of solution. That is, the family became both the unit of observation and the unit of treatment.

Family therapy is based on the idea that the family can be seen as if it were a rule-governed system. For instance, an observer might notice that when A nags, it is likely that B will withdraw. The observer might also note that when B withdraws, A will probably nag. The observer might then say that A and B appear to follow this rule: if A nags, then B withdraws, and when B withdraws, A nags. Which comes first—nagging or withdrawing—depends on when the observer starts describing what he observes. With the enlarged boundary, the problem is not simply that "A is a nag" or "B is withdrawn." Rather, the problem can be seen as involving the interaction between nagging and withdrawing.

Family therapy is based on the idea that human systems are fluid, evolving, and changing. Within this particular context, there is no clear connection between "cause" and "effect." There is no way for either participants or observers to know whether (a) A's nagging caused B to withdraw or (b) B's withdrawing caused A to nag.

Family therapists tend to believe that when there is a shift in the nature of interaction among family members, this makes it possible for the individual member to change, and when the individual member changes, the rest of the family will be affected in turn. The context or environment must also change to accommodate the individual's original change. That is, if A stops nagging then B will probably stop withdrawing, and/or if B stops withdrawing then A will probably stop nagging.

However, as we all know, stopping an undesirable behavior is not easy. A will find it far easier to substitute a different behavior for the nagging than to simply stop nagging, and B will find it easier to do something different rather than stop withdrawing. Although A and B might not be able to see it, an observer will likely notice that there are times when A and B interact without either nagging or withdrawing. These nonnagging, nonwithdrawing behaviors could be used to change the nag-withdraw pattern. For instance, any one of A's typical nonnagging behaviors toward B might be substituted for the nagging when B withdraws; then B will likely respond without withdrawing.

The interrelationship between an individual and an environment led family therapists to the idea that a small change by A can be followed by disproportionately larger changes in A's family. For example, if A starts being nice to B and B responds positively, then this shift can create a chain reaction within their context. The more often A and B repeat this positive exchange, the more likely it is that this will influence C and D. This is called "ripple effect."

With an enlarged boundary around solutions, family therapy points to the idea that developing solutions—within the interactional context—depends on at least one of the involved individuals doing something different from his or her predictable behaviors.

As you can easily see, this is a radical departure from the traditional assumptions about individual mental health problems and treatment. It is easy to see that, compared to traditional individual psychology, the systemic view tends to be more optimistic about the potential for change.

This way of looking at the child and his/her social relationship has a significant impact on the way we provide child welfare services: Instead of looking at the individual child or the parent as the focus of change, we look at them as a resource for change.

The clinical practice of family therapy is significantly different from an individually oriented treatment model. The family unit is seen together rather than the individual with symptoms. Even when an individual client is treated, the therapist looks at the individual problems within the family context and looks at how the individual client is influenced and is affecting the rest of the family. Therefore, the treatment focus is on the family interaction patterns, and not on the individual psyche.

SOLUTION-FOCUSED THERAPY

Solution-focused therapy, a model of intervention developed and described by de Shazer (1985, 1988, 1991), myself (Berg & Miller, 1992) and our colleagues at the Brief Family Therapy Center in Milwaukee, is yet another treatment model that is considerably different from others.

It is based on some of the same interactional and systemic ideas as family therapy, but from that philosophical base, it departs significantly in a number of different ways. The most important difference is the view of change. Unlike the family therapy view that the family unit is motivated by pressure to maintain a homeostatic balance and maintain its boundaries, solution-focused therapy views change processes as inevitable and constantly occurring.

Like the Buddhist view that stability is nothing but an illusion based on a memory of an instant in time, solution-focused therapy views human life as a continuously changing process.

Focus on Solutions, Not on Problems

Solution-focused brief therapists believe that it is easier and more profitable to construct solutions than to dissolve problems. It is also easier to repeat already successful behavior patterns than it is to try to stop or change existing problematic behavior. Furthermore, they believe that activities that center around finding solutions are distinctively different from problem-solving activities. For example, the activities a worker may engage in to "protect a child" from his abusive or neglectful parent are quite different from those designed to "build safety" for the same child. What the worker does becomes even more different when he looks for and finds instances when the parent is already successful in insuring the safety of the child, even a little bit and even if it occurs only occasionally. Getting the client to repeat her successful method of child rearing is easier than trying to teach her totally new and foreign skills. This clearly is an easier and simpler type of solution.

Clinical activities that help to enlarge and enhance those behaviors related to exceptions to the problem provide the keys to finding solutions. The following are important components of this model.

Pre-Session Change

Frequently, clinicians encounter clients who report that since they have been contacted by the child welfare department to set up an appointment for a home visit, things have changed markedly and positively. When the staff of the Brief Family Therapy Center paid close attention to this phenomenon (Weiner-Davis, de Shazer, & Gingerich, 1987), they found that about two-thirds of their outpatient clients report some form of positive change in the direction they were seeking help for in therapy. Understanding and paying attention to such pre-session change leads to quick solution finding since the initiative for positive change has already started to work and the family already knows that they need to do in order to bring about even small changes.

Unless they are asked, most clients do not think such changes are significant enough to report, or they appear very small compared to the massive problems they are faced with. Most workers ignore such pre-contact change or they brush it aside as a "resistive" maneuver or as "minimizing" the seriousness of the problem.

Since the client has already made positive changes, goal-related changes, the worker's task is to amplify, reinforce, and help the client to repeat the positive changes they have already made on their own. Later chapters will show the techniques for implementing this approach.

What are Exceptions?

Exceptions are those periods when the expected problem does not occur; for example, when a child who "fights all the time" or "lies all the time" has a period when he is cooperative and honest. When a great deal of attention is paid to the interactional patterns around those periods, that is, what mother does, how the child starts to be cooperative or honest, what else goes on when he "behaves," and so on, such activities provide clues to what the client needs to do more of. Initially, to most clients, exceptions to problems seem unimportant or insignificant. However, when both mother and son can find ways to repeat the behaviors that surround exceptions, the problematic situation becomes less overwhelming and more manageable, and eventually disappears.

Change occurs in different ways: emotional, perceptual, and behavioral. When feelings about a problematic situation change, it is possible to make a perceptual shift, followed by different behavior when a problematic situation is perceived as positive, one can make behavioral changes and think and feel differently about the problem, thus creating different emotional reactions; when one behaves differently, emotional and perceptual changes follow. These are as interconnected and interrelated as A's nagging behaviors are related to B's withdrawing behavior, making it difficult to figure out which came first, the familiar "chicken or egg" dilemma. Instead of trying to figure out whether it was the feelings, the thoughts, or the behaviors that came first, paying close attention to how the client made the shifts is much more profitable. Repeating these small but successful behaviors forms the basis for solutions. They become the keys and clues for solutions. Details on how to tickle such trigger points are described below.

Deliberate and Random Exceptions

In our study of exceptions, we found that there are two types of exceptions that clients describe: deliberate and random.

A deliberate exception is one that the client is able to describe in a step-by-step fashion. An example of such an exceptions is: "I forced myself to get out of bed, forced myself to go downstairs, made coffee, got the kids off to school, and forced myself to get out of the house. It helped me to feel a little bit better about myself." Since the client can describe what she did, she can repeat those behaviors that helped her to feel better. Clearly the task for the client is to "do more of it."

When random exceptions occur, either the client is unable to describe her successes or she attributes them to someone or something as if she had no control over the episode. For example, the client will describe the day she felt a little less depressed as, "I have no idea what made the difference on Wednesday. I just woke up feeling better," or "It was the day a package arrived from my grandmother who raised me," or "When I woke up the sun was shining and I felt better." Since the client sees herself as having had no part in creating the exception, it is difficult for her to replicate it. Such situations call for a different intervention or task, one that predicts what kind of day she will have tomorrow. Then, a review of what she did to have "a good day" will provide directions on what to "do more of."

Another example of random exception involves a client I met in Oslo, Norway. A man in his late thirties had suffered from chronic headaches for six years. He reported that medical tests had uncovered no physiological explanations for his headaches. When asked about the times when he did not suffer from headaches, the man reported that when he put his left hand over his head to "shield it from the atmosphere," he was fine. But it was difficult to keep his hand above his head all day long because he could not get any work done. Even though this was clearly an exception to his chronic headaches, it was not a useful one because it was impractical. After further discussion, the man realized that when he played his guitar, he completely forgot about his headache and was able to concentrate on his music. It happened that he joined a band that practiced together once a week. His wife concurred that he was back to his old self, spontaneous, likeable, and laughing like a little boy, which was what had first attracted her to him. Putting his hand over his head was not a realistic or helpful exception, but increasing his musical practice was realistic, as well as socially acceptable.

Goal Setting

Termination should begin with the first meeting between the worker and the client, if the worker is to avoid the interminable cases prevalent in child welfare. FBS cases, more than any others, require clear goal setting if the worker is to avoid the dangers of habitual contact, possibly only terminated by emergency intervention to protect the children.

There are two different ways to negotiate goals. One is through setting a defined number of sessions, 20 or 30 meetings, or two meetings a week for five weeks, and so on, or by determining a period of time over which to meet, 30 days, three months, six months, or a year, for example. Such an approach has positive and negative aspects. The positive aspect is that both parties will know clearly when the end of the contact will occur and work toward that date. The negative aspect is that both parties can just "buy time," waiting for the end to come, with no clear sense of what has been or needs to be accomplished.

The second approach is the one I advocate: having clear, well-defined goals that can be described in a specific manner and are concrete and behavioral enough that they become outward indications of the internal changes that are occurring.

The "miracle question," a goal-setting and solution finding

technique, will help the client specify how things will be different once the problem is solved (see Chapter 6). Clients are asked the following question: "Suppose a miracle occurs tonight while you are sleeping and the problem that brought you to the attention of the child-welfare service is solved. You will not realize right away the problem has been solved. What do you suppose you will notice different the next morning that will let you know that there has been a miracle overnight?" This "miracle picture" is used as a road map for figuring out where the client wants to get to and for suggesting what needs to be done to accomplish the desired changes.

The model described here is often characterized as being "goal driven," that is, the therapeutic activities that both client and worker engage in are always related to goals. Unlike the medical model, where the professional becomes an expert whose role lies in diagnosis, solution-focused therapy follows the client's lead in setting goals for the treatment and in laying out plans for the client to implement. For instance, when the client says to the worker that one of her goals is to "get the social service out my life," the worker agrees with the client that it is a worthy goal to work towards, since the ultimate goal of the worker is to successfully terminate contact with the client. When the goals are laid out by the client and not defined and imposed by the worker, the client is more likely to be committed to achieving them.

Guidelines for setting "workable" goals for FBS will be described in more detail in Chapter 5.

Worker Role

It is already clear that solution-focused therapy calls for drastically different activities on the part of the worker. The worker-client relationship is conceptualized as the product of interaction between the worker and the client, thus forming a unique but temporary system engaged in finding solutions to the client's problem. When the task is accomplished, the relationship ends.

The worker is actively involved with the client in looking for pre-session change and exceptions to the problem, in constructing imagined solutions, and in asking questions that will help the client to discover her own solutions. By asking what appears to be a simple question, the worker is intervening in the family system. Since the solution is generated by the client and not introduced into the system from outside, change occurs rapidly, and the likelihood of a setback is greatly reduced. Our study indicates that as time goes on, the "ripple effect" appears to create long-term, positive influence (Kiser, 1988).

Three Rules

1. If it ain't broke, don't fix it. Simple observation will reveal that A and B are not always nagging-withdrawing-nagging. Even the most chronic of troublesome patterns is absent now and then. Sometimes, in fact, the problematic pattern is only a very small part of the client's life. Except in rare circumstances, even abusive parents do not abuse their children all the time. There are frequent periods, which sometimes last for a long stretch of time, when that same parent can be loving and nurturing, and can behave in a very competent manner.

Determining what is "not broke" and, therefore, does not need fixing, is subjective at best and not scientific. Workers need to have a very broad view of what "works" and "does not work," since much of what causes the client to come in contact with child-welfare services can be viewed as stemming from extreme differences in culture and lifestyle.

2. Once you know what works, do more of it. Solution-focused therapists believe that paying close attention to periods when the client is competent, nurturing, and responsible is much more productive than focusing on pathology, since such positive behaviors form the basis for strengthening families and promoting good parenting skills. When each exception is studied carefully and who does what, when, where, and how is considered, it will usually reveal a successful pattern, however small. Because these are behaviors the client has already mastered, either recently or in the past, it is fairly easy for the client to replicate those exceptions. Increasing the period of existing success as well as recognizing the competency of the FBS clients, is much easier than mastering new and different behaviors. Such an approach results in FBS clients feeling empowered to solve problems in their own unique ways.

3. *If it doesn't work, don't do it again; do something different.* If one were to ask B "why do you withdraw?" chances are that he would say that he is trying to get A to stop nagging. As far as he can see, withdrawing or getting away is the only reasonable approach; he might say that he only needs to withdraw more often or more effectively in order to get A to stop nagging. However, B is reinforcing A's nagging. Although the old adage of "If at first you don't succeed, try, try, again" might work in some situations, solution-focused therapists will maintain instead, "If at first you don't succeed, try something different." Thus, if B wants A to stop nagging, he might first notice times when A is not nagging him and notice what she is doing instead. Then B should notice what *he* is doing when A is not nagging. For instance, B might notice that A never nags when he is holding her hand or when they are talking in the kitchen over a cup of coffee. If B responds to A's nagging with nonwithdrawing behavior, such as holding her hand or talking in the kitchen, then it is likely that A will cease nagging. In fact, the chances of A responding to B with her non-nagging behavior will likely increase. Thus, A and B would have changed from a nag-withdraw-nag-withdraw pattern to a nag-withdraw-hold hands-kiss, more-talk-more-kiss sequence.

2

The Initial Stage

WHAT THE ASSESSMENT IS
DESIGNED TO DO

THE MOST FREQUENT misuse of the assessment is when it is a laundry list of all the things that are wrong with the client. For example, you will often see a detailed account of what a poor childhood a client had: how she was abused, grew up in a foster home, has no contact with her mother, and was "hooked up" with shady characters who used her. This assessment may go on to describe how she had four children by different men, and how she neglects and abuses her children now.

Such a list implies that the client is doomed to fail in life and, thus, even before the first visit, it is easy for the worker to take a negative view of the client. Such an attitude will not help the client, especially since we all convey what we think and feel in subtle, nonverbal ways, as well as the ways we phrase our comments and questions. Once we start to feel overwhelmed by problems, we tend to look for ways to justify our failure, and so we describe clients as "unworkable," "unmotivated," "lacking insight," "resistive," "shopping around," "not ready for change," "yes, butting," and "minimizing." It is easy to see how this works as a self-fulfilling prophecy.

What is most important to remember is that the client may not agree with the laundry list of problems at all but may instead have his own ideas about what the problem is. If this is the situation, we have a clash over what the problem is and what to do about it. It is not hard to imagine that such clashes can lead to "client resistance," "yes, but . . . ," "avoidance," "passive-aggressive behavior," or "noncompliance."

A way of avoiding such "resistive" or "uncooperative" client behaviors is to conduct an assessment in such a way that a list is made of activities that both worker and client need to do. Making a master plan to replace the unsuccessful problems-solving attempts with more successful ones, aiming for small changes, and making a list of activities that will move you towards the easiest way of finding solutions are all much more helpful ways to "assess" clients.

As you read this book, you need to bear in mind that the assessment is best thought of as a map that you and your client contract together in order to figure out where you both want to get, rather than a list of what is wrong with the client. Since you will be the guide, perhaps you need the map more than the client does. Assessment is your preparation for the trip.

PRE-ASSESSMENT INFORMATION

Before the Intake

Before meeting with the client for the first time, gather all the data you have about the new case. This may include information from medical sources, courts, school systems, relatives, church, neighbors, or from a previous contact with a protective services intake worker, the referral source, your supervisor, or the previous case worker.

When you are reading the records from previous contacts, try to figure out what was previously tried with this case and, also, what was suggested but obviously not tried. All the information about what *not* to do is contained in such records. Reading between the lines will give you some clues about how the previous worker and the client got along and perhaps some ideas about what the previous helper got along with the client or where they failed. Obviously you do not want to repeat the previous helper's mistakes. You do not want to do "more of the same" things that did not work.

Using the Information You Have About the Case

It is useful to keep in mind the following questions as you sift through information you already have about a family that you have not even seen yet.

1. What mental picture do you have of the family?
2. What emerges as the strongest issue about the case?
3. What would the client see as the most important issue? How would you find this out?
4. Who would be the most influential person in this family, and how would you enlist this person's assistance?
5. What is it that you should not do with this case? What mistakes did the previous helper make?

Once you answer these questions, you will begin to get a mental picture of the case as well as some ideas about what might be the best approach.

Being Open to Change

Even if the client has been in treatment many times, it is always possible that the family's situation has changed since the last time. Sometimes a new partner, a new job, a new place to live, another child in the family, or a summer respite from raising children alone, can change the family situation in a positive way, but it can also create more stress. It is very useful for the worker to be open to any possible changes, both good and bad.

It is best to assume that life is always changing and that each encounter with social services may be different. Even for "seasoned" clients, and even if their lives seem the same, contact with you will be very different since you will use a paradigmatically different approach to treatment.

THE HOME VISIT

Things to Keep in Mind

As you get ready for the session in the client's home, keep the following in mind.

1. It is an important part of your task to set the tone for a friendly, positive atmosphere during the home visit. Assume that you are accepted, and be casual and relaxed. The client is likely to take cues from you.

2. Use normal, everyday, conversational language in a friendly, soft tone, and use neutral words and phrases. If at all possible, use positive words. Instead of hammering away about "problems," use words like "troubles," "difficulty," "hassles," or "solutions." Imagine yourself talking to a neighbor over a cup of coffee around the kitchen table, while remembering that you are at work and your conversation is a tool for change.

3. In your interactions with clients, learn to trust your own judgment and intuition. As long as you maintain a respectful stance with the client, your incomplete information or your lack of detailed knowledge about the client can be turned into an asset. For instance, by acknowledging your lack of information, you can make the client the "expert" on the details of the situation.

4. Learn to use yourself as a tool for helping clients — use your common sense, your observational skills, and your senses.

5. Always maintain a positive, hopeful view of clients and your work with them. When you are hopeful you tend to convey that to them in many subtle and nonverbal ways. Most clients are sensitive about picking up cues from what you don't say as well as what you do say. Learn about subtlety in interpersonal contacts, and use it to help clients improve their lives.

6. It is essential that you pay attention to parents as well as to children. Many parents are isolated and lonely and can become

PRE-ASSESSMENT WORKSHEET

Family Name: _____ Case # _____

Referral Date: _____ Workers Name: _____

Referral Source: _____

Reason for Referral: _____

_____

Family Members   D.O.B.   Occupation   Relevant Information

_____

_____

_____

_____

_____

What Worked: _____

_____

_____

What Has Not Worked: _____

_____

_____

Comments:

easily threatened when the worker pays an inordinate amount of attention to their children.

7. When parents make complaints about their children, it is a clue to you that you need to find ways to compliment their parenting. All parents become defensive about their parenting. When they become defensive, it is easy for them to look for explanations for what went wrong and it tends to be the child who is held at fault.

Things to Do

There are positive and negative aspects to conducting a session in the client's home, and your skills will be what turns the negatives into advantages. Conducting a session in the home is a lot like being a guest in the client's home, with the important distinction that you will be making suggestions and at times demanding that she change the way she runs her life. The following points will ensure that treatment sessions conducted in the home will have a positive impact.

1. Make an appointment for a visit. Ideally, ask for permission to enter the client's home, as this will shift the perceived balance of power away from the "invasive professional." When invited, act like a guest, since that is what you are.

2. It is important that you feel comfortable in order for your client to feel comfortable. Wearing "smart" clothes that may get soiled if the home is not clean will create a barrier between you and your client. When the sanitary condition of a home is bad, you can comment on it by saying things like: "The landlord is not keeping up with his job of fixing things around here," or "The landlord should do a better job of keeping this place clean." These comments make a point without pointing the finger at the client.

3. Like a good guest, make a comment about something nice or attractive, or something they have clearly put a lot of effort into. Remember that a client's home is her personal space; you may not agree with her taste, but it is important to respect it. Ask which is her favorite chair and where she wants you to sit.

4. Make comments about any family photos you see; ask questions about who is who in the family. You may gain some important information through this. Remember, your relationship with the client is a professional one and not a social visit. Learn the fine boundary between a courteous, friendly, and professional visit and a personal relationship where the client becomes your "friend."

5. Make the family members the expert on something you see in the home, such as a pet, woodworking project, knitting, puzzles, fishing/hunting, or accomplishments indicated by awards or plaques.

6. Schedule the home visits for a fixed time and day of the week. This provides some structure to what may be a disorganized life.

7. Bear safety in mind, both yours and your client's. If you do not feel safe, you will not relax and you will not create rapport with your client. Do whatever you need to do to feel safe. You may have to raise the issue with the client. On those rare occasions when there is clear physical danger to yourself, *leave immediately*. Whatever information you need can be obtained later when you return with an escort.

8. Distractions such as television, telephone, children running around, dogs, neighbors, or visitors coming in and out can be a nuisance, but you can also think of ways to use them. Do not hesitate to ask clients to lower the volume on the television or the noise level in the home, but phrase your request as one for help, since you can get easily distracted. The following are some examples of how to phrase such a request:

> "It would be very helpful for me and I would hear you better and give you full attention if you would turn down the volume a little bit." Or "I am having trouble concentrating. It would be very helpful if you could make the children speak in lower voices." Most clients are cooperative and willing to adapt.

The negative side of the home visit is that you are in someone else's space or territory. Workers are not as familiar with "the lay of the land" as the client, and have to adapt to the way clients do things, such as patterns of eating, standards of housekeeping, sanitary conditions, level of noise and activities, and so on. It is important to remain flexible.

Management of Angry and Hostile Clients

Some workers find dealing with the angry and hostile client the most stressful and difficult aspect of their work. It is prudent to pay attention to anger and hostility since these emotions can alert the worker to a potentially dangerous situation.

Since most clients are "referred" by other programs (such as Child Protective Services, Alternate Care Programs, family court), they are supposedly "voluntary" to the FBS program. However, most clients feel coerced into "voluntary" participation for family-based treatment in order to get something else they really want, such as reunification with their children. Therefore, you may encounter some clients who are openly angry and hostile toward workers, even though they may have initially agreed to participate. Although overt anger or hostility can cause stress, it is often easier to deal with and manage than a passive-aggressive style.

The client's anger usually can be attributed to the frustrating circumstances the client is in, but in some cases it may be due to a chemically altered state or mental illness. This book will address only those situations that can be managed by treatment approaches, and not by legal or other physical means.

When working with hostile clients, it is vital that you ensure your safety. Since I assume that you are familiar with various techniques of defusing emotions, hostility, and violence, you are advised to refer to them.

If it is known that a client has been hostile to other workers, ask what has helped to diffuse the anger in the past; you may want to try the same. Also, find out what the other worker tried that *didn't* work; it is equally important to know what *not* to do. If someone is paranoid or suspicious, do not argue with her; agreeing with how she sees things does not mean that you support the perception. Distract an emotionally charged or agitated person from an upsetting topic by gently changing the subject, or by turning your attention to another person or activity that is less upsetting to the client.

In order to turn a difficult situation into one that is helpful to the client, always look for ways to use the situation to help the client feel more comfortable, empowered, and in control of himself. The following are some helpful hints.

1. Normalize the client's anger and hostility toward you. Allow her to vent her anger and frustration for a few minutes. Don't rush to defend yourself or your department but listen quietly and attentively to her complaints.

2. When the client begins to calm down, indicate your admiration for her fierce independence and desire to protect her privacy. Explain that it is an indication of her desire to run her own life and you absolutely agree with her wish not to be told what to do. Then, casually ask if she has always been such an independent person or is this something new for her. Where did she learn to be such an independent-minded person?

As you are saying this make sure that you sound sincere; the best way to do this is to really believe what you are saying. This is called "reframing," a technique borrowed from family therapy. Sit back and watch your client calm down and start to cooperate with you.

3. Next, quietly ask her in what way can the worker or the FBS program help her remain independent and protect her privacy. Do not get bogged down with complaints; after a brief period of venting, move on. Some examples are: "So, what would it take you to keep your privacy?" or "Absolutely, I agree with you. So, what do you have to do so that they will leave you alone to run your own life?"

4. Distance yourself from the target of her anger. Since you are agreeing with the client's perceived cause of anger, make sure that you do not identify yourself with that same target. For example, if the client is angry at the Children's Hospital for having reported her for a suspicious injury her child sustained, do not defend the Hospital or the doctor, but put distance between you by referring to them as "they" or "the doctor

at the hospital," and so on. This gives you some room to maneuver later on.

5. Give the person space to move around, allow him to leave the room or to walk out of the house, meet in a larger room of the house.

6. Do not feel compelled to stay in a potentially violent situation. Allow yourself easy access to an exit.

Paying Attention to the Client-Worker Relationship

Most FBS programs have many "clients," that is many service providers and funding sources have their own agendas, which they impose on families. These are often not what the client wants for himself. At times, it is very difficult to figure out who is most invested in change and who should be the main players in solving a particular family's problem. The person who should be most concerned about solving the problem may turn out to be the least bothered; instead, someone else may be more willing to do something about finding solutions. Such confusion partly stems from the way we use the term "client," since it does not give us a clue as to who is most invested in working to solve the problem. In this section, I will describe some useful ways to assess the worker-client relationship.

Not all worker-client relationships are the same, as most experienced workers know. Assessing what kind of relationship the worker has with each client helps him to know what to do and what not to do in order to enhance client cooperation and prevent worker frustration.

The worker-client relationship is never static; it is fluid, ever-changing, and dynamic. As you read this section, I suggest that you review some of your current client relationships.

The worker-client relationship is the foundation on which the task of problem solving is built, but the relationship itself does not *create* change. Many beginning workers expect dramatic change following a "heart-to-heart" talk with their clients. It is a naive notion to expect that a change follows a discussion of one's feelings or a tearful session with a worker; this is only a beginning. Doing something about the problem creates change, not talking about it.

Many workers, counselors, and therapists have found the following notion of assessing professional relationships very useful. Keep in mind that this is not a description of the client, but rather the nature of the relationship at a particular point in time; the worker and the client share equally in forming and maintaining the relationship.

Visitor Relationship

The visitor relationship exists most often when the client is ordered or referred by the court, job training program, probation officer, school, family members, or employer; therefore, they often come to the worker's attention with the referring person's, and not their own goals. Clients may or may not agree with the referring person's idea of what the nature of the problem is or what should be done about it. When they disagree, such clients are often thought to be resistive to acknowledging their problems, or to be refusing to take responsibility for the problems, to be minimizing the extent or the seriousness of the problem. They are thought to be difficult or impossible to work with. When your caseload is made up entirely of such clients, it is easy to imagine how it contributes to staff burnout.

There are clients whose main goal is to avoid getting involved in the helping system, since from their point of view there are no complaints or problems that they need help with. If they feel a problem exists, they think it will not change, or, more frequently, they do not see the connection between their problem and any solutions the worker may offer. Their real goal is to end the contact with the workers as soon as possible and to be "left alone."

With reluctant clients, the worker's task is to:

1. "Join" the client's world view as described in the case example below. Being sympathetic to her predicament also helps.
2. Find ways to influence, shape, and mold the client so that she can identify problems and possible solutions to them. Once

the client perceives that there is a problem, she can be engaged on a different level. This sometimes happens only after pressure from child protective services: "Change things or you risk losing your children."

3. Agree, as far as possible, with client's idea of what the problem is for her.

Some clients will take longer than others to progress, depending on the worker's skills in accomplishing the three tasks outlined above and the client's experience with previous helpers. The more pressing the problem is to her, the more likely she is to take steps. The following is an example of how a worker "joined" a client, helping her to identify the problem and a possible solution.

Case Example

Worker: Do you have some ideas about what we can do to be helpful to you so that your family can stay together?

Client: I keep telling you people over and over that somebody reported me when there is no reason to.

Worker: Do you have hunches or guesses about what he or she might think you need help with?

Client: Damned if I know. The police were here the other day because they thought the children were left alone. It's probably my mother who called. Well, she always meddles in my life just because I got pregnant when I was 17. She still thinks I'm 17 and treats me like it. She is convinced that as long as I keep my boyfriend, I will always be the worst mother in the world. I don't care what she thinks anymore. Fred isn't going anywhere, and you are not going to take my child and give him to her.

Worker: We don't want to do that, and we don't want to keep coming here, either. We have better things to do than to come and bug you. What do you suppose you can do so that your mother will not keep calling the Department and you will be left alone?

Client: There is nothing I can do. I tried everything with that woman.

Worker: I am sure this is no fun for you. You have better things to do than have to put up with me coming here. Any idea about what you will have to do to keep your mother from bugging you like this?

Client: She wants me to get rid of Fred, but as I told you it's not going to happen.

Worker: Obviously your mother is not convinced of how committed you are to Fred. Obviously she does not see the good things you see in Fred. What do you think will convince your mother that Fred is good for you?

Client: I guess I will have to let her come here more often and maybe not tell her about our fights. She thinks I am her baby and she has to protect me from Fred. He gets rough with me and the kids when he drinks.

Worker: You must love him very much. What do you suppose other people like your sister or your best friend would say is good for you?

Client: They think I shouldn't take all that crap from Fred. He gets me so mad sometimes but he is a good father, and he is good to me when he doesn't drink or use drugs. He goes to work every day.

Worker: So, what do you have to do so that you and Fred get along better and your mother will leave you alone and not call us?

Here, the temptation is for the worker to jump in to either rescue the client, as her mother repeatedly does and fails each time or lecture her on what a bad influence it is to have Fred using alcohol. The worker wisely realized that if he were to take either step, he would only be doing "more of the same," with disappointing results.

In contrast, by "joining" with her, that is, by acknowledging that she must have good reasons to stay with Fred despite everyone's advice to leave him, the worker focused on what the client needs to do (proactive), instead of how she needs to defend herself against criticism (reactive). The worker not only avoided being dismissed as being "just like everybody else," but also got the client to start thinking about what her responsibilities. This approach of asking questions is more likely to result in the client's own recognition that there is a serious problem between herself and Fred.

The best approach the worker can take at this stage of the relationship is to acknowledge the client's frustration and the many intrusions she has endured, and to point out her strengths and her good intentions.

Complainant Relationship

This type of relationship exists when the client views his relationship with the worker as limited to providing information on his problems. Although affected by the problem, the client does not yet see himself as having a part in its solution. However, the client usually perceives his role as giving detailed and accurate account of patterns of behavior, historical narratives, speculations about causes, and possible solutions to the problem that someone else might perform.

The client usually sees himself as an innocent bystander who has to endure the difficulties others inflict on him. Since he does not see himself as the cause of the problem, the client is likely to see the burden of solution as lying with someone else. The grandmother in the previous case is a good example of a complainant relationship. Perhaps out of feelings of helplessness or because she sees the problem as solely her misguided but stubborn daughter, the grandmother makes frequent complaints to the Social Services. But she is not yet willing to do something about her own part in the strained relationship with her daughter.

It is easy to misread the complainant-type relationship as a customer-type, which will be discussed next. Remember that the level of distress the client feels or expresses is not sufficient indication that she is ready to take steps to solve problems.

Since the client is not yet at the point of seeing himself as involved in solution finding, the worker needs to be sympathetic and to thank the client for the helpful information he has provided. The worker needs to acknowledge the client's suffering and to applaud him for "hanging in there" despite the difficulty of the situation. The worker should compliment the client on having the commitment and willingness to seek help for the troubled family member.

The following conversation indicates how one client conceptualizes her difficulty, and it is a good example of a complainant type of relationship with a client who sees the solution as outside of what she can do.

Worker: What do you think will help you to get along with your daughter?

Client: It's not me. Lisa will have to get it into her head that she gotta behave or else I'm going to kick her butt.

Worker: Sounds like you have a big problem on your hands. So, what would it take for Lisa to start listening to you?

Client: That child will have to start listening to me and stop saying things like I beat her. I didn't threaten to kill her! She runs around and tells everybody I mistreat her. She lies and shoplifts but everybody thinks she is a cute little angel and says it's all my fault. I didn't do anything wrong.

Worker: It's pretty tough raising a teenager alone. So, what do you think it will take for Lisa to start listening to you so that you don't have to get mad at her?

Client: She will have to find out how good she has it before she will start to listen to me. I keep telling her what will happen to her if she doesn't listen, that I will put her in a foster home. I think she has to get good and scared before she realizes how good she has it at home. I think that's the only thing that will work with Lisa because she has always been that way.

Worker: What do you think Lisa would say would be helpful to her?

Client: I don't know; she never talks to me. She has this attitude that she knows everything and that she can do anything she wants to do when she wants to do it. I keep telling her that I'm not going to stand for that, but she never listens to me. I'm not going to take it anymore.

Because the client has not yet owned up to her desire to improve communication with Lisa but, rather, sees the problem as belonging to someone else, it is too early to start talking to her about what she needs to change. For now, however, the most helpful approach for the worker to take is to sympathize with her difficulty and to initially agree with her goal of seeking help for her daughter.

Until the client has indicated that she is ready to take steps to solve her problems, any suggestions the worker makes should be limited to thinking, analyzing, or observing the *presenting* complaint. Since the client is already doing many of these activities, she is likely to cooperate with the worker.

Customer Relationship

In the customer-type relationship, both the client and the worker may not yet be very clear about the goals (see Chapter 5 on well-formed goals). However, in many ways, both verbally and nonverbally, the client indicates that she is interested in and committed to solving her problems, regardless of whether or not she believes she is responsible for them.

So how can the worker tell when the client has the customer-type relationship with him? It is apparent when she says things such as "My life cannot go on like this anymore. Something has to change"; "It's time to turn things around. But I can't do it alone. Can you help me?"; "Nothing I tried seems to work. I need someone to point me to some new ideas."

There are clients who, for whatever reason, have reached a point of saying, verbally and nonverbally (such as gestures, tone of voice), that they are ready to do something to change their lives. Clients can reach this point by various routes, some good and some not so positive. When someone reaches this point, she can develop a fairly positive, cooperative working relationship with a worker. Following is an example of a client and worker in a customer-type relationship.

> Worker: What do you think it will take for you to have all these people out of your life?
>
> Client: I have to get my act together; get rid of my boyfriend, concentrate on taking care of my kids, stay clean, take care of my business, keep going to CA [Cocaine Anonymous] meetings, and talk to people when I get upset.
>
> Worker: What do you think it will take to stick with it? You said you don't handle boredom very well. You know taking care of the kids can get pretty boring at times. What do you need to do so that you can stick with it?
>
> Client: I'm not sure, but I have no choice. I can't ruin my kids' life. They belong with me. I don't want no stranger to raise my kids.

Even when you have someone as motivated as this client, you need to stay focused on the goal and keep reminding the *client* about the goals.

The Hidden Customer

Many FBS clients can be thought of as "hidden" customers, that is, they may not initially be willing to deal with the problem that got them referred to the program, but they may be willing to become a "customer" for what they consider is important. For example, a client is referred because the public health nurse has determined she needs some parenting classes. At the time, the client seems to have agreed. However, when the FBS worker actually sits down with her, she gives the impression that she is more preoccupied with her strained relationship with her boyfriend than with parenting issues. It is prudent for the worker to "cooperate" initially by agreeing to discuss what the client thinks is urgent. It is my clinical experience that when the worker "cooperates" with the client first by allowing her to become a "customer" for what she is interested in, the client-worker relationship is greatly enhanced.

Finding the "Other" Customer

One of the most common characteristics of FBS cases is that there are multiple systems involved in a single case. Frequently the real "customer" is someone other than the client. Funding bodies, special programs that target certain client populations, political activist groups, and perhaps your supervisor or the program director have set personal and programmatic goals for the client. Because *they* have set these goals, it is crucial that the worker view them as customers. If this is not done, it is easy for the identified client and the worker to become confused about whose goal they should work toward. The goals of these "other" customers are all legitimate and appropriate; the skill for the FBS worker lies in making clear all agendas and helping the client sort them out.

As mentioned earlier, finding out the real "customer" for change is crucial for ensuring the successful outcome of the case. It is pragmatic and productive to utilize the energy and urgency for change that is already present instead of trying to create the motivation for change when there is none. For example, if the court seems to be the real "customer" for a case, be sure you work with the court system personnel in such a way that their goals for the case are addressed.

WHAT TO DO IF OTHER
SYSTEMS ARE INVOLVED

It is important to take other systems into account in a case—the school, the visiting nurse, the public health service, the courts, other treatment personnel, even the grandmother who raised the children and lives upstairs. As you identify the nature of the systems involved in a case, the following information will be useful to you.

1. Make sure that you get the client's permission to talk to other systems in order to avoid duplicating services.
2. Make sure that you contact the other worker to let him or her know that you are working with the family.
3. Elicit the treatment provider's perception of the problem.
4. Find out WHO did WHAT to solve WHAT problem. Find out what WORKED and what DID NOT WORK. This information will direct you on what to DO and NOT to do.
5. Figure out a cooperative way to work with the other worker.
6. Find out what is the goal for the other helping person.
7. Make sure that he or she is not more motivated to change the client than the client is to change herself. In other words, make sure that you are not your own "customer" for your own services.

3

Defining the Problem

EXPERIENCED WORKERS know that there can be many answers to the question "What is the problem with this case?" The problem as defined by the referring person may well differ from the client's definition of the problem, which, in turn, may differ from your definition. Since the definition of the problem will dictate what you will do to move toward its solution, it is worthwhile paying close attention to this question.

In negotiating the definition of the problem to be solved with the client, it is important, whenever possible, to stay close to the client's own definition, since he is the one who will have to make the necessary changes. In addition, it is vital to negotiate a problem that can be solved given the client's current situation and resources. Asking yourself the following questions helps to organize your approach to the case in these early stages:

1. What is the referring person's view of what should be done with this family?
2. What is the client's view of what should be done?
3. What is your view (or the team's, if you are a part of a team)?

4. Is there someone else playing a key part (e.g., child protection worker, school social worker) at this stage? If so, what does he or she think needs to change with this family?

Case Example

The school called the protective services agency asking for an investigation into the possible neglect of seven-year-old Shranda. They reported what appeared to be a chronic state of neglect: Shranda appeared unhealthy and often was unbathed. She seemed withdrawn, listless, easily distracted, disinterested in her surroundings, and at times obviously hungry. They reported that the mother, Martha, did not respond to their letters and did not show up for conferences. Since the family had no phone, the school could not contact her.

The protective services report indicated a marginal level of neglect, nothing grossly abusive, but certainly the family's functioning had been going downhill in recent months. Martha reported that she had been very depressed since she found out that she was pregnant again by her boyfriend James. Her mother and sisters had repeatedly warned her against James, who had recently been released from prison, having served time for his terrible abuse of Martha. The pregnancy was the last straw, and she now faced the difficult decision of what to do about it.

She agreed that things had not been going well for her and her two children and that she spent a great deal of time in bed, didn't prepare meals for them, and just didn't have the energy to do anything. Since there was no substantiated neglect, the case was referred for treatment at the community mental health center.

Since the client's view of the problem plays the most important part in forming the solution, the worker spent a considerable amount of time trying to establish Martha's view of the situation and what she wanted to do about it.

When sympathetically approached, Martha was finally able to agree with the school's concerns. She had been a good mother, once, and she should have been doing a better job. Even though initially she had been reluctant to accept the outreach of the protective services worker and the school social worker, Martha began to acknowledge that she had a problem and that she needed help.

The teacher's initial concerns about Shranda had turned out to have much larger implications. Instead of being a simple neglect case, the problem was related to Martha's pregnancy, which, in turn, exacerbated the strained relationship between Martha and her mother, and also forced Martha to make a decision about her relationship with James. Martha felt caught in the middle, wanting to maintain both relationships but realizing it was not possible.

WHO IS MOST CONCERNED
ABOUT WHAT PROBLEM?

Assessing who is sufficiently concerned, upset, or bothered enough to do something to solve the problem is vital. A number of common signs can help to make this distinction:

1. Strong emotions, both positive and negative, expressed as the problem is discussed.
2. Nonverbal cues that match the words of upset and concern; that is, the person's statement of the problem is accompanied by appropriate emotional reactions, such as upset posture, leaning forward, or eager facial expressions.
3. Verbal responses that indicate an investment in change, such as "Something has to be done"; "It can't go on any longer"; "This is terrible"; "Nothing I tried works"; "I don't know what to do anymore."
4. Some expression of willingness to do something about the situation.
5. Expression of hopefulness about the situation, a belief that things can improve with help.

The person who is most upset about, uncomfortable with, or indignant about the situation is the one most likely to take some steps to solve the problem. It is easier to follow where the energy is than to try to create energy where there is none. If this person is in a position to take steps to solve the problem, then that is useful and helpful to know.

For example, if the assessment is that Martha's mother is the party most upset about Shranda's not being taken care of properly, or Martha's letting herself go, or James' ruining Martha's life, then it may be more productive to work with the mother than with Martha. If, on the other hand, your assessment is that Martha is most concerned about the state of her life, it will be more productive to work with Martha.

If you are the person who is most concerned and upset and most invested in change, then it is clear that your client is a "visitor" or a "complainant," and not a "customer" for change. Maintaining a balance between being objective and yet empathetic enough to understand the client's pain is not easy, but it is essential for successful treatment. If the worker feels overwhelmed, upset, and finds himself blaming one part of the family more than others or being more sympathetic to one or two family members, this may be because he is over-invested in solving the client's problem. There are many possible reasons for this, including unresolved issues on the part of the worker. Whatever the reason, though, it is crucial to acknowledge this and to seek consultation or supervision.

Case Example

Let us return to the case of Shranda. Interviews with various people concerned about Shranda's welfare indicated that Martha was most invested in making a decision about (a) what to do about her pregnancy, (b) what to do about her relationship with James, and (c) what to do to take care of Shranda. Now the worker needs to formulate a tentative picture of what the next steps in the treatment plan should be.

Adding this information to what you already know about this case so far, the worker should be able to answer the following questions:

1. What is the "official" problem with this case?
2. What is the client's view of the problem?

3. What is your view of the problem?
4. Who is most invested in solving the problem?

The next step in the ongoing assessment is to identify the resources that you can build on.

WHAT ARE THE STRENGTHS
IN THIS FAMILY?

It is easy to become overwhelmed by the scope of problems of the families that come in contact with the social services, in general, and FBS cases, in particular. Frequently, these families are thought to lack even simple problem-solving skills. When the worker believes this, it is easy for her to become overwhelmed and discouraged.

However, my experience with such clients as the homeless (Berg & Hopwood, 1991) is that they are very resourceful and have an enormous degree of resiliency and strengths (Lum, 1992; Saleebey, 1992). Individual client's problem-solving methods may be different from those of the mainstream culture, but the solution perspective allows the worker to see the potential strengths and resources in these unique and diverse techniques. As indicated in Chapter 1, identifying strengths and successes and enhancing them are much more respectful of the client and less exhausting for the worker than dealing with weaknesses. For example, take the case of a 22-year-old single parent with a five-year-old child. This woman was able to raise a child while she herself was still going through adolescence. It means that she has had to solve hundreds of the large and small problems of daily living at an young age. This reframes her as being a competent woman, rather than an irresponsible, unwed teenage mother.

History of Previous Contact
with Social Services

If there is a record on file of a previous contact, even if it was not an intensive one, asking about it, in a casual and neutral way may produce some useful clues about the client and her willingness to work with you.

Examples of useful questions at this stage are:

> "It seems that the school is very concerned about your daughter, and I understand that you have had some meetings with the school. How helpful were those meetings? What would you say the school did that was most helpful for you?"
>
> "It seems like many people are concerned about your daughter. What do you suppose you did to get them to see that they didn't have to be concerned about you?"
>
> "The record indicates that you have had dealings with our department before. What did the worker do last time that was most helpful for you? Least helpful?"
>
> "You have had some contact with the public health nurse before. Could you tell me what about your meetings with her you found most helpful?"
>
> "You have two children in school. What do you think the school did that was most helpful for you and the children?"

Asking these questions will:

> 1. set you on the side of the client and thus put you in a position to evaluate her previous contacts with the helpers;
> 2. set you apart from them but also give you information about the client's view of her previous contact, and what was viewed as helpful or not helpful;
> 3. show clients that you are willing to do what would be most useful to them; and
> 4. convey to the client that you are willing to recognize her past successes.

If the client seems negative about her prior contact with professionals, refrain from defending the previous helpers and, whenever possible, agree with the client—for the time being. Asking the client's perception of her past success in handling various "helpers" establishes that you think that she was successful in the past.

Family History: Genogram

As we mentioned earlier, any assessment information should be gathered with an eye towards its usefulness in figuring out what to do or where to go next. The genogram is no exception. Make sure that information from the genogram will be useful in relation to both the client's and the worker's goals.

A genogram is an attempt to map out family coalitions, alliances, historically significant events, life change events, family myths and rules, and other significant issues that may have an impact on the client. Detailing such events helps to place the current problems within the context of the family history as well as the social context of the family. It can also give the worker very useful clues to hidden issues.

The timing of asking for this historical information is crucial. Some clients may view it as being intrusive when they do not see how it relates to their problems. Yet, talking about the family history can be a useful tool to help the client become curious about herself and her problems. Obviously you need to use your clinical judgment and common sense regarding timing. If you feel awkward initiating a discussion about family history or if the client acts as if it is a strange request, it is probably better to postpone going into it. Unless the discussion makes sense to the client, her curiosity is unlikely to be stimulated in a way that opens the possibility of new understanding and change.

The genogram can reveal some important patterns in the family: good and bad family myths, hidden ghosts, the belief system, the family structure, who "takes after" who, and so on. These patterns may have significant impact on the client's beliefs about her past and future and may explain what has shaped client's view of herself.

Family history can be a neutral, matter-of-fact issue or an emotionally charged one. You may need to gather information over several sessions, especially if the client seems reluctant to talk about her family. Reluctance could be an important clue as to what might be a sensitive issue. If so, do not force the issue before the client is ready to talk about it. During the assessment phase, the most important job is to motivate the client to do something about the situation that got her into contact with the helpers.

Remember, family history is a reflection of how the *client* sees her family; it is not always a reliable or accurate portrait, and, therefore, it is negotiable. In retelling the story, clients modify, change, invent new myths, and drop certain pieces. In other words, this history is the client's construction, it is not made up of true or false statements, and with each retelling the story becomes more real to the client. Accept the client's perception of her family. Stone (1988) describes the wonderful ways people invent and reinvent family history to fit their needs. The worker therefore must be selective about the use of family history, that is, she must use it to shape a positive view of the client and her family of origin.

Many FBS clients have strained relationships with their family of origin; thus, they may isolate themselves from a potential source of support. Frequently, the client recognizes that she was determined to be different from the way she was raised but is upset at herself for doing the same things her mother did. Find areas where the client has achieved a degree of autonomy, and support the hard work it took to do it. When she feels successful, it is easier to be positive about her ties to the family of origin.

The following information should be obtained through a series of conversations, rather than by using a form. Encourage the client to elaborate on her view of the family, and make sure that your questions are phrased in such a way that the client does not answer with just "yes" or "no." Allow the client room to elaborate in her own words. You will learn not only about the client's use of language, but also her story of how she fits into the family.

1. What is the client's view of her family of origin? The client may see her family as a positive force in her life and, therefore, as a potential source of help. On the other hand, she may see their relationship as a source of friction and a problem to be avoided. If her view is positive, the worker can emphasize this aspect and become curious about how she chose to adopt the positive traits from her family. If her view is negative, the worker can ask how she was smart enough to know how *not* to adopt those traits. The client can be asked how successful she feels she has been in what she has set out to accomplish. Give the client credit for having achieved a degree of success. Many workers become upset when a client distorts her family history and believe that must be confronted. One can lose an important opportunity to help the client reshape her story in a positive direction by insisting on absolute accuracy. It is better to accept the client's perceptions and work to influence them toward what is good for her. What follows is an example of how a worker can reframe a client's "dysfunctional" family of origin experience.

Client: My parents always told me that I would never amount to anything. They never showed me affection, never kissed or hugged me. I guess my mother grew up in a family that didn't show any affection. She just didn't know how to help a child to have self-confidence. I believed for a long time that I will never be anything good. Then I started to rebel against that and told myself that I would show them who I really am. But then I did my rebelling by running away, getting pregnant, skipping school, and getting into trouble with the law and stuff like that.

Worker: So, how did you figure out that you were different from what they thought you were?

Client: I just knew it inside. I just wanted to prove to them that they were wrong about me, and I was going to show them who I really was.

Worker: How did you do that?

Client: I wanted to be a good mother to my child, a better mother than the one I had.

Worker: Where did you learn to do that?

Client: I just watched other people do it and then imitated it.

Worker: That takes a lot of commitment to your child and also a brain to figure out what to do. How did you do that?

Client: I was going to be a different kind of mother. I swore that I would never make my child feel inferior, and I never do. I never tell him he is a piece of shit.

Worker: You mean you had to teach yourself how to be a good mother? You must love our child very much.

When the client is successful in changing even a little bit of the family myth and making a positive move (for example, toward her image of what a good mother is) such departure from the family belief system needs to be supported and encouraged. It helps the client to know that it is possible to shape her own history in a way that is consistent with who she is.

2. *Where are the current alliances and resources?* Alliances among family members can be discovered by asking questions, such as who visits whom and how often, who is the person that maintains contacts with family members either through phone or letters, where does the family meet, who is the "switchboard" for gossip and information that gets passed among the family members, whom does the client call when she needs help? Knowing this information will help the worker know who might be the most influential person to involve in order to make changes.

It is also useful to know who, among the relationships the client maintains in her family system, has been most helpful to her and in what ways. It will help both the worker and the client to figure out what she does to maintain such a supportive relationship and what she needs to do more of to keep it. If the client has lost valuable support, what would it take for that family member to help her again? What are the rules for keeping the support, and is it worth the emotional price she pays for it?

Worker: You mentioned that your grandmother has been an important source of help to you in the past. What do you suppose she would say it would take for her to help you again?

Client: I suppose she would say I have to cut off James for good this time and not take him back.

Worker: That sounds like a tough choice. So, how will you

know which is more important to you, keeping James or keeping your ties to your grandmother?

Client: It is tough to decide. I want my grandmother to be proud of me and to see my kids. They need that. I'm not sure about James. He has not been good for my kids. They are afraid of him, and they shouldn't be. I don't know which is good for me, it's hard to decide. I guess I want both but I can't have both.

Worker: It sure is tough to decide. Is there some way you can do both?

Client: I'm not sure. I never thought of that.

3. *What is her family's view of her relationships with men?* This seems to be the most frequent source of conflict for FBS clients. The major reason for emotional cut-off and tension between a young woman and her family is around the issue of men she chooses. Therefore, important questions to ask when dealing with such women are: Does the family approve of her choice of men? Do they think she has done well with men over the years? What do they think she needs to do? What do they believe is the reason why she is attracted to men they believe mistreat her? If her family is angry at her choice of men, obviously it is because they care about her intensely.

What follows is an example with a woman whose family disapproves of her boyfriend:

Worker: What do you suppose your mother would say she wants you to do about your boyfriend?

Client: She thinks all men use me, that I don't know my own mind, and she's always telling me what to do. It really bugs me that she thinks I am so stupid. She really never let me choose my own friends, just because I made a mistake when I was 17.

Worker: What do you suppose will convince her that she does not have to worry about you now?

Client: Nothing will. Any guy I have, she always finds something wrong with. She is never satisfied. She didn't do so well herself, married to a drunk. She has such a boring life, and I think she lives her life through me. I keep telling her that I am not going to live my life for her and then we get into big fights. That's when she calls the social service.

Worker: What small things do you suppose she has to see you do for her to believe that you can take care of yourself?

Client: If I don't ask for money from her. If I can manage my money, I suppose. She thinks I give my money to my boyfriend so that he can buy his booze.

Worker: Suppose you did not ask for money from her? How do you suppose she will react differently with you?

Client: She might nag a little less.

Worker: What difference would it make for you when she nags a little less?

Client: Then, I could enjoy talking to her. I don't want to cut off the apron string altogether. I just want some room to be my own person.

Worker: How will you know you have become your own person?

Even when there appears to be an overwhelming conflict that dates back to the client's adolescence, with the worker's help it is possible for the client to begin to figure out what she has to do to achieve her goal in a constructive way and to stop blindly rebelling against anything her family advocates.

4. *What is the client's sense of her own autonomy?* Does the client think she has done well as a parent, as a daughter, as a professional, or as a person? For example, does she believe she has done a better or a worse job of parenting her child than her mother did with her? What kind of parent does she want to be? How is she similar or different from her mother? Information on

these questions will give you a good sense of the degree of her autonomy and the separation between generations. The worker needs to pay attention to the smallest indication of independence and autonomy and to enlarge on it.

> Worker: You mentioned that it is important for you to be a different kind of mother than your mother was for you. How did you figure that out?

> Client: I remember when I was a child I used to think how I will never be like my mother. I will never hit my own child — I will always listen to her, praise her, respect her wishes, and spend time with her and things like that to let her know that she is important to me.

> Worker: How successful would you say you have been?

> Client: I am still learning and I have a long way to go.

> Worker: What do you suppose your mother would say what kind of mother you are to your child?

> Client: She would say I am doing a pretty good job.

> Worker: How do you explain that?

> Client: I worked very hard. I go to classes, I read a lot, I watch other people who I think are good parents and listen to them. Mainly I would say I listen to others.

This client needs to be complimented on the intelligence and thoughtfulness behind her success. Whenever the client breaks a family pattern by making a conscious effort to change her behavior and increase her sense of independence, she needs to be supported and given credit for the hard work she has done.

If she thinks she has done a better job than her mother had done with her, how did she learn to do that? Has she taught herself or did she learn from someone else? Whom did she learn from? Either answer could be an opportunity to compliment her — for having given a lot of thought to the issue, which is a sign that she cares about her children, or for having had enough

4

Developing Cooperation

MOST THERAPEUTIC MODELS and treatment approaches emphasize the importance of the client-therapist relationship and see it as
the essential ingredient in any professional relationship. Obviously, when the relationship is positive, everybody tends to see things
in a more positive way, which therefore enhances the chances of
good results.

However, the client-worker relationship should be viewed as a
means to an end, rather than an end in itself. Whereas a positive
working relationship enhances client motivation and helps them
to be more cooperative and open with the worker, it would be a
mistake to believe that the relationship itself is enough to change
client behavior. For change to happen, the client needs to make a
perceptual and cognitive shift and to do something that is behav-
iorally different from what he has been doing.

WHAT IS "JOINING"?

Joining is a term borrowed from family therapy, which I will use
here to describe what the worker needs to do in the engagement
phase in order to establish a positive working relationship. It is
primarily the worker's task to reach out to the client, project a

warm and positive feeling, and give the client confidence in the worker's trustworthiness. This is done through a variety of verbal and nonverbal, subtle and not-so-subtle cues and activities.

The ultimate goal of "joining" the client is to make your job easier. When clients believe you are interested in them and want to work with them, they are more likely to cooperate and work with you and to make changes. The ultimate beneficiary of your "joining" with the client is the client himself.

How Can the Worker "Join" the Client?

1. Before meeting the client for the first time, put yourself in his position and imagine what you would want a worker to do for you. Remember to set aside your personal feelings about the client and to take a detached but a curious stance with him.

2. Avoid professional jargon. Use simple, everyday language. Avoid bureaucratic or provocative words like "individual," "residence," "level of education," "socioeconomic status," "perceive," "evidence," "abuse," "report," "investigation," "accusation," "allegation," "perpetrator," and so on. These are best saved for discussions with other professionals. Instead, use terms that clients use: "home," "neighborhood," "person," "concerns about you," "to make sure you are doing okay," "phone calls," "to help you take care of your child," "understand," "hurt," and so on.

3. The first meeting sets the tone for positive contacts later on. You need to use friendly, positive words. Give some thought to what kinds of things the client would be defensive about and make sure that you handle those carefully. Say things like, "My job is to keep the peace in the family. It is obvious that your family is going through some tough times, and I wonder how I can help"; "It is not easy raising three kids alone. I imagine sometimes you feel like giving them away. I wonder how you do it."

4. Look for key words or idiosyncratic ways the client uses certain words, such as "fussing" or "bothering," or "discussion" for "argument," and try to mimic their use. For example, if a

client says that the kids' "fussing" bothers her the most, you can incorporate her words by asking, "So when your kids fuss, what have you tried that worked?" Keep track of at least three words that the client uses frequently, any unusual way of using certain words, or any words that are emotionally charged. Pick up on these words and repeat them when you talk to the client. For example, a client describing how she felt when the police showed up at her door accusing her of beating her 13-year-old daughter said:

Client: I had to scrape my self-esteem off the floor. All I could do was just burst out crying.

Worker: So after the crying stopped, what did you do to scrape your self-esteem off the floor and stand up for yourself?

5. Behave as though you accept his way of doing, seeing, and explaining things, even though it may not seem logical or realistic to you. It does to him. Imagine yourself standing behind your client and peering over his shoulder and see what he sees.
6. *Do not* confront the client directly or do things that will make him defensive. Always avoid getting into debates or arguments with clients. It works better when you take a "one down" position. Say you are "confused," or "don't quite understand," and ask for further clarification. Most of us, and clients are no exception, like to help others and want to show how much we know.
7. Let the client be the "expert" on his problem and circumstances. As far as possible, do not tell him what his "problem" is; let him tell you. If the client disagrees with your view, you take on the added burden of proving and persuading the client to agree with you. This is a position a worker should not be in, since it will likely lead to the worker becoming more of a "customer" than the client and thus to her working harder than the client to solve the problem.
8. Instead of expecting the client to accommodate to your way of thinking and doing things, remind yourself to adapt to his way of thinking and doing things. It makes carrying out your

tasks a lot smoother and will be less work for you in the long run.

9. During the early phase of your work, compliment the client frequently for anything positive she is doing.

10. When treating the family, do not take the child's side but support what the parents are trying to do with their child. Remember, your task within the FBS is to empower the family, and when the parents feel competent and successful this benefits the children in the long run.

11. Talk to the client in a way that he can relate to. If you have someone who is very concrete and has difficulty in understanding abstract terms, you need to talk about what is important to him in a very concrete manner. If you have someone who is visually oriented, use visual words, such as, "So what do you need to see different in your life that will tell you that things are getting better?" If your client uses auditory cues, use words like, "So what changes will you listen for that will make you tell yourself that things are better?" Someone who is kinesthetic will use many words related to actions. Respond in kind by saying, "So when you feel better about yourself, what will you be doing that's different from what you are doing now?"

As you collect information, answer the following questions yourself.

1. What is important to this client?
2. What would make sense to him?
3. What are his problem-solving strategies?
4. What are his successes and failures around this particular problem?
5. How does he see the problem? How does he explain that he has this problem?
6. What is he willing to do and what will he not do?
7. What resources are there to draw on — the extended family, neighbors, church, special friend?

The answers to these questions will give you some ideas on how to adapt yourself to your client. When the client thinks you respect and validate his ideas, he will respect and validate your input.

Obviously, your job does not end with "joining." When you feel that the client is beginning to give you credibility, then your job is to influence him in such a way that he does what is good for him.

Case Example

The adoptive parents of an eight-year-old were extremely angry at his school for having listened to a lie that their child told a teacher about how he was beaten, given no food, and was tied to a bed. The school had promptly called the protective services, the parents were "investigated," and the case was referred for counseling.

The parents were angry with the school for having reported them and at protective services for investigating and referring them for treatment, which implied that they were doing something wrong. The child had many emotional problems and had been placed in eight different foster homes by the time he was seven years old. Their lofty and loving intentions had not led to the blissful family life they had imagined, because their son was causing so much havoc. They were angry about having to be in counseling when the real problem was the school taking the side of the eight-year-old.

These parents needed to be complimented for having taken on a tough job of parenting such a difficult child. What's more, even though they felt that they were "unfairly treated by the system," they were still willing to come to counseling and try to solve this problem. When the worker was sympathetic to their plight, they relaxed considerably and became much less defensive. Only then, the parents were able to think about what they needed to do so that this will not be repeated.

Frequently, the crucial issue is whether the client feels her position is accepted and her feelings are validated as legitimate and not whether the client is responsible for the problem or not.

Case Example

The parents of a 15-year-old girl disagreed over discipline and threatened each other with divorce over their disagreement. They told the worker that their 15-year-old was "seeing" a 26-year-old man every day, went to his house and ate dinner there. When at home she was on the phone to him all the time. Apparently the disagreement was over whether seeing this man was good or bad for their daughter. The mother said, as did the daughter, that it was better than having her run wild in the streets, while the father had "no use for him" and at times he was "ready to kill the guy." They said they needed help in deciding what to do.

The parents were complimented on agreeing to take steps toward a solution, such as coming to talk to the FBS worker and making sure that they do the right thing for their daughter. The worker told them that she could see they loved their daughter very much and that each had very valid points. Once acknowledged and given credit for their genuine concerns for their daughter, the parents were able to move on to how to integrate both of their concerns into action.

Case Example

28-year-old Betty was very angry at the social worker for "taking my baby for no good reason" and was in no mood to cooperate. She was hostile and ready to fight with anyone from social services, court, or the hospital. Even though it was not that hard to see that she was very pained by the loss of her baby, she expressed her anger at the system more readily than her pain.

Realizing that the first task was to join the client, the therapist was very sympathetic and said that it was certainly understandable, and he did not blame her for being angry. The therapist went one step further and mentioned that it was clear that Betty was indeed a strong person who believed in doing the right thing. (It would have been a serious mistake at this point to argue with Betty about the facts surrounding the removal of the child and defend the other professionals' actions. Sometimes it may be necessary to postpone knowing "the facts" about the details of the case such as Betty's since one assumes that there was a good reason for removing an infant like Leroy. But the temporary posture the worker takes of "not knowing" makes it possible to establish the positive working relationship with the client.)

Betty started to relax a bit and then started to give more details of the circumstances that led to the removal of the child. Leroy, age two, was placed with Betty's mother. Betty has been visiting her son "unofficially," without the knowledge of the social services.

She went further to explain that because she believed that she didn't "do anything wrong," she refused to comply with court requirements for drug tests, counselling, and visitation under supervision. After a considerable period of venting, Betty eventually decided that she is now ready to do all the things that the court required her. It took some time because of court hearings, which were postponed several times, but Betty eventually accomplished her goal of getting Leroy back home.

DEALING WITH RESISTANCE

What Is "Resistance"?

Many types of clients have a reputation for being "resistive." Some examples are teenagers, alcohol and drug abusers, mandated clients, school or protective services cases, or clients who come to treatment under coercion by their family or spouse. They are thought to willfully refuse to cooperate with the agency, to be sneaky, evasive, and often angry and hostile toward social workers and other helpers. There is a lot of "evidence" and experience that give weight to such bad reputations. Some clients are indeed unfriendly, reluctant to give information, evasive, and at times downright nasty, hostile, or threatening to workers. What is there to do when faced with such a situation?

Since we have taken a consistently systemic view throughout this book, we need to apply the same concepts to this situation as well. When we are willing to change our lens and are open-minded about looking at unfamiliar landscapes, a new perspective is available to us. Instead of the "resistive client" against the "impartial, objective social worker," we can see also a clash of cultures and life styles with opposing goals and expectations. What makes the need for such a change of lens more clear is that the large system representing the community (such as the legal, medical, educational, or social services) often "barges in" uninvited and threatens the very survival of the smaller system by pointing out what they are doing wrong, telling them what to do, and demanding that the small system change its views, values, and life style.

The belief systems, values, and priorities of the community agencies are frequently very different from those of the client system, especially if there is a clash of cultures.

When cultures, values, and goals clash, it can resemble a territorial conflict, with each side holding onto their way of doing things. The client believes that his is the better way, and, unless he decides that changing is in his best interest he will cling to "his" way as a way of asserting control over his life. Even though we as workers do not like the idea, the community often uses the treatment system both to enforce its values and as a tool for the purpose of social control; therefore we become the agent of such control. It is important to recognize our dual roles of being the change agent and the enforcer of the society's values and belief system.

Family or client resistance is strongest when the larger system tells the smaller system what it is doing wrong and demands and insists that it adopt different ways of doing things.

Therefore, the worker's task is to build cooperation and increase effectiveness. You can see why it is a big task; but it is one that can be rewarding in the end.

Ways to Build Cooperation and Decrease Resistance

1. Have an open mind about the client and be prepared to give her "the benefit of the doubt."
2. Put yourself in her shoes and look at everything from that point of view.
3. Figure out what is important to your client at this time, and see this view as a valuable asset that has served her well over the years, although this very point of view may get her into trouble now and then. Maybe when she recognizes the pros and cons of her attitude, she may be more willing to change.
4. Do not argue or debate with the client. You are not likely to

change her mind through reasoning. If this approach was going to work, it would have worked by now.

5. Check once more how realistic your expectations for the client are, given her limitations and circumstances. You may change your views later on, as will the client.

6. Look for the client's past successes, however small, ordinary, or insignificant. Ask how she achieved them. This question alone becomes an indirect compliment.

7. Look for any small *current* successes and ask how she accomplishes them and what it would take her to repeat or expand these to other parts of her life. It indicates your confidence in her ability to solve problems.

8. Look for positive motivation behind the client's behavior and comment on it. She will begin to believe it herself.

9. If you have to choose sides between the client and other social service systems, choose to be on the client's side until proven wrong.

10. Be willing to apologize to the client for any mistakes or misunderstandings. It takes strength, self-confidence, and professional integrity to be willing to apologize, but, paradoxically, it gives you credibility and power in the relationship.

11. If a client is not home or is unavailable for meetings, it may not necessarily be a sign of resistance. For many families being on time is not considered important. The client may not mean it as a personal affront to you.

12. Always use a gentle and soft voice, use positive, not negative words, and nonthreatening gestures.

13. Most clients respond better when you provide services that are related to immediate problems such as, housing, diapers, food, day care, getting the gas turned on, and so on.

When Nothing Works with a Family

Even when you make all the right moves, it is still possible that you will not succeed in getting all clients to be cooperative. The reality is that there are limits to what the worker can do to influence the client. "You can bring a horse to water, but you can't make it drink" is a good proverb to remember.

Occasional failures to "reach the client" and establish a positive relationship remind us that we must learn to accept our limitations. An important point to keep in mind is that the client has a right to self-determination but must also accept the consequences.

EMPOWERING THE CLIENT

The 19th-century "Mary Ellen" case, which initiated the child welfare movement in the U.S., was based on the notion of "protecting" the child from those around her who "abused and neglected" her. Therefore, it is logical that child welfare policies and the workers who implement these policies tend to view their primary responsibility as "protection of the child." Many child welfare programs are designed to do just that, and there is a need for them.

What Is "Empowerment" of the Client?

The notion of "empowerment" of the client seems almost to be a new slogan taken on by the FBS field in recent years. Therefore, it may be useful to review this notion and how it is practiced in FBS.

Empowerment of the client is an attitude based on a certain philosophical view of human problems and solutions. The treatment model described in this book empowers the client and is based on the notion that the client is competent to make choices that are good for her. As stated elsewhere, empowering the client is not the same as condoning the antisocial or illegal, or unhealthy belief system or behaviors. Neither is it the same as "enabling," which has developed negative connotations in recent years through its association with the drug and alcohol treatment field.

The empowering practice begins with the following:

1. The basic belief about the client-worker relationship is that it is a collaborative, joint venture between the client and the worker. It means that the worker is not an expert who decides what is good for the client or what steps she will take to imple-

ment these procedures, but instead the client participates and collaborates with the worker in these processes.

2. It is assumed that the client is competent to know what is good for her and her family.

3. It is further assumed that the client has the ability to solve problems and has solved problems in the past.

4. The client determines and negotiates the goals for the contact.

5. The client participates in the treatment procedures and selection of options that are suitable for her since she is assumed to be the expert on what is good for her, her life, her body, and her family.

6. The technique of complimenting the client is an expression of these assumptions about the client.

7. The emphasis on exceptions to the problem assumes that the client does solve problems on her own. Interviews are designed to uncover such solutions and successes.

8. The client is in charge of the termination of contacts.

9. It is an approach that respects the client's autonomy and personal, familial, and cultural boundaries, thus, it is less intrusive.

The most important thing to keep in mind is the concept that clients need to feel in control of their lives as much as possible. Client participation in goal setting and solution finding allows them a voice in determining the course of their lives. This is a very respectful way to work *with* clients, not *for* them. The more success they have, the better they will feel about themselves. Following is an example of empowerment in action.

A single mother had a great deal of difficulty controlling her children. She came to the attention of the FBS because one of her children was molested by a babysitter. The mother felt criticized by various helping professionals for not being consistent and not being able to follow through with the rules she set. She felt constantly overwhelmed by the children's problems: failing in school, behavior problems, a chaotic home situation. She was always tired and under stress. The children needed protection from her

ex-husband, who in the past had been physically abusive of her
and the children and was suspected of sexually abusing a daughter, yet she felt helpless to do anything. The children were out of
control and needed structure, consistent discipline, and follow
through to provide them with a sense of security.

By chance, the FBS team found that the mother was amazingly
successful as a supervisor of the housekeeping department of a
large motel chain. She received frequent promotions because she
was effective as a supervisor, loved her work, and was good at it.

Based on the empowerment philosophy, the team decided to
explore how her ability to supervise could be translated into being
a mother. The team decided to help her see herself as a supervisor
of her children. Effective "supervision" of children requires basically the same skills and approaches as those involved in her job:
being clear about expectations in concrete and behavioral terms,
reinforcing positive behaviors, giving frequent and consistent
feedback, and when appropriate, enforcing the natural consequences. The result was very positive.

In this example, the first task of the worker was to start seeing
this mother as a competent, effective person and to start looking
for her strengths. The imagined solution the team came up with
for this family was for the mother to start to "supervise" the children with clear rules and expectations and consistently follow
through with praise, limit-setting, frequent evaluations, rewards,
and punishments. All of these techniques she was already using
effectively on the job. The team discovered that, in her mind,
"parenting" was something entirely different from "supervising."
Therefore, the team kept referring to her task in the home as
"supervision" and "management" of her children.

5

Setting Goals and Making Contracts

UNCLEAR GOALS INVARIABLY lead to long-term contact. They also cause the worker and the client to become easily frustrated with each other, which frequently ends in mutual blame and unplanned termination. Of the hundreds of cases I have consulted on, supervised, and taught about around the world, the most common reason for therapists, counselors, and social workers to feel "stuck" is related to unclear goals.

Negotiation for goal setting between the worker and client starts as soon as the client comes in contact with social services. In fact, it would not be overstating it to say that the termination must be negotiated while the worker is trying to get to know the client. At the time of the very first contact with a family, the child protective services worker must be clear about what the purpose of her first home visit is, whether it is to be an investigative or a therapeutic one. Although this seems obvious at first, it can easily be confusing. For example, only about 30 % of the cases where there has been a complaint against the family actually turn out to have some basis for further investigation. This means that the other 70 % of the cases are potentially treatment cases. This means that the remaining 70 % are routinely closed with no further service even though there clearly are problems related to the family

63

functioning and child safety issues. These closed cases become repeat callers. When the goals are too rigid and followed only by the legal definition of the abuse and neglect the worker misses an opportunity to intervene therapeutically. Many workers tend to see a dichotomy between the investigation and treatment as if they are separate activities. I contend that investigation can be therapeutic when conducted appropriately, while treatment can be investigative when necessary. Therefore, the investigating worker can behave in such a way that his activities are therapeutic, that is, by healing and restoring the client's confidence in herself and thus influencing the client in making changes, however small.

From the beginning of contact with a family through termination the worker must keep a steady eye on the goals negotiated with the client. This chapter will deal with contract negotiation, guidelines for setting well-formed goals, goal maintenance, renegotiation of goals, and ongoing evaluation of treatment goals.

NEGOTIATION OF
TREATMENT CONTRACTS

As most FBS workers know, not all clients who come in contact with the FBS programs are "voluntary" clients, even though they may have "volunteered" to accept the service. However, even the "involuntary" or "mandated" clients have some voluntary aspect to their contacts with the worker because even clients who meet with the worker because of a court order do not really have to do so; he has the option of taking the consequences of refusing to meet with the worker. It is useful to keep in mind this "voluntary" aspect of the "involuntary" client. It is the worker's task to find out what the client is willing to be a customer for. In other words, every involuntary client is a potential customer for *some* service, even though it may not be what the worker is interested in having the client want. All clients hope to attain some goals through their contacts with the social services, even if it is only to "get the service off my back."

Negotiating treatment contracts with clients who want the worker to stay out of their lives is very difficult at first, but not impossible. When these clients are handled skillfully, they can succeed in achieving their goal of keeping the FBS workers out of their lives. Essentially, the FBS share the same goal: getting out of the client's life.

Before you start negotiating goals, refer back to the description of "involuntary" clients who are "visitors" and ways to work with them (Chapter 2). Again, keep in mind where the client "is"; that is, if her goal is to "stay out of the District Attorney's office" or to "get the social worker off my back" or to "get my parents off my back," that is a perfectly reasonable goal. In order to achieve such goals, the client will have to make certain changes, such as getting up in the morning, going to work or school, coming home on time, cleaning the house, and so on, which are good for her. A reminder: You need to be clear about who your real "client" is, whether it is your funding source, the referral agent, your supervisor, or even you.

The following are examples of questions that can be used in the beginning phase of the contract negotiation.

Worker: I know that coming here is not your idea of how to spend an afternoon. Any idea of what you would like to get out of coming here that will make it worthwhile for you?

Client: Well, it was very hard for me to make the phone call. I was wondering on the way over here what I would have to tell you. I think I need help but don't know if you can help. My life is a mess.

Worker: Yes, I am sure it was very difficult for you to come here.

Client: Well, I don't know. I don't want people messing with my life.

Worker: You know, Anita, that's exactly what we want, too. We want to get out of your life as soon as possible. What do you suppose you have to do so that we stay out of your

life and leave you along? What did Mrs. K tell you about
that? We are wondering how badly you want to keep
your children with you.

Client: Real bad. I'm their mother and kids should live with
their mother.

Worker: We absolutely agree. We know that you love your
children more than anybody and you know what is best
for them. So how badly do you want to change things so
that they can come back to live with you?

In this exchange between the worker and client, the worker
sets a positive tone by assuming that the client wants the children
with her and explaining that he wants the same thing. Having
put himself on the client's side immediately, the worker proceeds
to negotiate what the client wants in order to achieve her goal of
keeping the children with her.

Taking a sympathetic stance with the client does not mean
condoning the client's neglectful or abusive behavior, it only means
that you are open minded and that the client will get a fair hearing. This approach increases the chance of the client being less
defensive and allows her to be more open and honest with you.
Clearly the client will test you many more times to find out how
much she can really trust you, given all the bad stories she may
have heard about caseworkers.

GUIDELINES FOR GOAL SETTING

The professional worker-client relationship is a purposeful one,
that is, it is designed to achieve goals of facilitating the client's
sense of success, not failure. Its success or failure will depend
largely on what kind of goals you agree on and what methods will
be used to achieve the goals. If you do not have clear goals, neither
of you will know when you have succeeded, and it will be difficult to evaluate the work you and your client are accomplishing. You and your client may already be quite successful without
knowing it.

Goals have two components: *what* you are aiming for and *how* and *what* you are going to do to achieve it. When these guidelines are followed, you and your client are likely to find the paths and methods that will enhance success.

1. Goals must be important to the client.

We all know that unless someone wants to change, it is impossible to force change. And, since it is the client who has to make the needed changes, it is more prudent for the worker to agree with what the client wants to change rather than tell her what to change, if this is at all possible.

The goals must be meaningful to the client and she must view the achievement of the goals as having some beneficial and positive results for her. For example, her involvement with the FBS may result in her child behaving better, getting her son away from a gang, increasing her child's chances of success in school and in life, feeling successful as a parent, having her child returned from a foster home, and so on.

For example, what the client wants most might be for the worker to get out her life and not come around to "bother" her. If this is the case, it is indeed a good goal. The worker's job is to be able to close the case and do it without jeopardizing the safety of the children. Therefore, the worker and client want the same thing, that is, to "stop meeting like this."

Case Example

Worker: So what can I do that will be helpful to you?

Client: I want other people to stop messing with my life.

Worker: I think you are absolutely right. We want the same thing for you. We want to get out of your life as soon as possible. So what do you have to do so that we don't have to meet like this?

Client: I suppose you have to think that I don't mess my kids, which I don't.

Worker: I am glad to hear that. I also have to be able to report to my supervisor that you are managing your life in such a way that there is no danger of your child getting hurt. I am sure you want the same thing also. So how badly do you want to get rid of me? (A scaling question would be very useful here. For instance, "On a scale of 1 to 10, where 10 means you will do damned near anything to get rid of me, and 1 means you will just sit around and wait for something to happen, where would you say you are at today?")

Even though what the client wants does not come from the kind of motivation that we might wish, it is always much better to begin with "where the client is" and move on from there rather than trying to change her mind. When the worker "cooperates" first with the client, it is much easier for the client to "cooperate" with the worker. Once the client recognizes that the worker has a genuine respect for what she feels is important and good for herself and her children, it is easier for the client to move beyond insisting on her own agenda. Clients are very sensitive about subtle, nonverbal messages, therefore, be sure what you do is what you believe about your client.

Case Example

Linda, a mother of four children ages 14 to 4, was very angry and defensive when the worker first met her. All her children were removed when the oldest, Tish, reported physical abuse to the school. Because they could not find a foster home that could take all the children, they were placed in three different homes. Linda was court ordered to receive individual and family counseling with the children. After six months, Tish was the first to express desire to return home.

In order to gather information, we asked about Linda's contacts with various helping professionals. She described the family counseling she attends with 11-year-old Marcus as very upsetting because she somehow gets the impression that the counselor only listens to Marcus and not to her concerns about his poor school work and the trouble he's been in at school since he has been at the foster home. She also complained a great deal about various foster parents who treat her "like I am a criminal or something." She didn't like the social worker who "kept telling me what to do, like I was ignorant or something."

Linda is a big, barrel-chested woman, who talked with a tough booming voice, saying, "I tells it like it is and not beat around the bush." It was easy to believe her and, at the same time, to be easily put off by her. In addition, her "disciplinary" measures were very harsh and unrealistically demanding of her children. Her view of the world was that one had to fight everything and everybody just to survive: "Don't let nobody walk on you."

When asked the "miracle question" (see Chapter 6), she softened considerably and became teary-eyed, saying that she loved all her children, and she wanted all of them back with her but realized that she would have to do it with one child at a time. The worker agreed with her plan and realized how important it was for Linda to be a good mother. Picking up her plan the worker started to negotiate ways to implement her goals.

Worker: What would it take you to do that?

Linda: I have to keep going to counseling, keep visiting my kids, go to parenting classes, learn to keep my temper under control, and keep my job.

Worker: So what is the first step you need to take?

Linda: I want Tish to come home first because she said she now wants to come home.

Worker: What do you have to do so that it will happen?

Linda: We have to talk, really talk. I have to let her be a teenager and she shouldn't have to be scared of me.

The worker decided that Linda's immediate goal was to have Tish come home first and that her plan to have one child returned at a time seemed reasonable and realistic. In addition, she already was recognizing she and her daughter must be able to talk to each other without being scared. This was the beginning of the goal negotiation.

2. *Goals are described in social interactional terms.*

Truly "no man is an island," and this is particularly so for FBS clients because the very nature of their problem is defined in a social context. Determining whether a child is in danger of being placed outside the home, if a particular client needs parenting classes, even whether a child is being successful or not in school is decided according to a particular community's standards. Social workers are particularly sensitive to the interaction between the client and her social and ecological context and their influence on each other. Most FBS workers are acutely aware of this issue when negotiating goals with "involuntary" clients who must deal with a referring person who insists that the client must achieve certain goals from their involvement with FBS.

You will find that all clients will benefit when you can help them to formulate goals, as the following example shows.

> Worker: What do you suppose your daughter will say how you and she will get along better when you can talk to each other instead of fighting?

> Client: She will say I will listen to her and will see her side of the story and not jump on her. And I know I have to listen to her more, but sometimes she makes me so mad.

> Worker: So when you listen to her more what will your daughter do different that will let you know that it is working?

> Client: Maybe she won't scream at me so much.

3. *Goals must be small, simple, and realistically achievable.*

Contrary to our "common-sense" notion that big problems take big solutions, the solution-focused approach insists that even big problems can be solved with small, simple solutions. We frequently overlook the most obvious solutions, thus unnecessarily complicating the problem solving activities when we fix our eyes on the problems. How can you tell a goal is small enough? It is usually something the client can do immediately, within the next week or two. For example, for some clients, "getting a job" is too big a goal; submitting two job applications is small enough that he can do it immediately. "Quit drinking" is a big goal; going to one AA meeting is something most clients can do. For some clients, getting up early enough to get the children off to school everyday may be too big a goal, but perhaps one day would be manageable. The goals you help the client negotiate should be something the client can realistically do, given her difficult life circumstances. She needs more successes, not failures, in order to gain confidence in herself, and small and concrete successes enhance her chances of achieving larger ones. You may wonder how such a small goal can solve all the enormous, overwhelming problems the client has. You can imagine how the client would feel overwhelmed! But systemic theory says that a small change in one aspect of a client's life has a way of generating changes in other parts of her life — this is called the "ripple effect." We are taking advantage of this systemic phenomenon that occurs by allowing the inherent systemic nature of the family to take care of generating solutions.

Case Example

Sharon readily agreed to take Antabuse to control her episodic drinking binges, which put her children in jeopardy. The worker, alert to the fact that Sharon could not afford to fail one more time, asked about the details of the Antabuse program. It required daily attendance at a clinic located outside the city, which meant a daily bus trip with three small children. The meeting she was to attend was held from 2:00–3:30 p.m. everyday. This meant that Sharon would not be home when her seven-year-old returned from school. Clearly, the worker and Sharon had to come up with some other, more realistic plan.

4. Goals are described in interactional terms.

John Dunne said, "No man is an island." When a mother is depressed over a prolonged period of time, it affects her relationship with her child in a significant way. When a child is cranky, diffi-

cult to manage, and not easily comforted, it in turn affects the
mother's reaction to the child. For far too long the fields of social
work and psychosocial treatment have paid little attention to the
interpersonal and interactional components of human relationships, but focused instead on the individual psychological dynamics and the treatment of individual psychopathology. The FBS
model corrects this oversight: Since you are frequently in clients'
homes and are able to observe many things that clients may not
think are important enough to tell you, you can see these interactional dynamics at work. When negotiating goals with the client,
it is the worker's task to help the client state the goals in a way
that the client describes *with* whom as well as where the changes
will happen. An example of how you can help the client state the
goals in interactional terms follows:

Worker: What do you suppose will be the first small sign that
tells you that your daughter is getting her life together?

Mother: She will not talk back to me anymore, cuss at me, or
call me names. She will go to school.

Worker: So, let's suppose she does that, which I think will take
a while. What do you suppose your daughter will say
how you will be different?

Mother: She would say I will not nag her anymore. I will be
nice to her and we can go back to talk to each other again.

Worker: What will she say you will do instead of nagging at
her when she does all that: talk nice to you, not call you
names, go to school, and start to have a better attitude?

Mother: She will probably say that I will be more willing to
listen to her more, not call her friends up and check up
on her. She hates that.

Worker: When your daughter notices you are more willing to
talk to her, listen to her side of the story, and so on, what
would she say how things will be different between the
two of you?

This example makes it clear that, initially, this mother only thought about what the *daughter* would have to do to change. In the process of answering the worker's questions, the mother began to get some ideas about change *she* could make. It is no mystery that when the mother is more positive toward the daughter and respectful of her friends and her privacy, it will help the daughter feel that mother is more respectful of her. It will increase the likelihood that the daughter will respond more positively toward the mother, thus improving the relationship between the two. The strength of this kind of goal negotiation is that the mother may get the idea that perhaps she can start the positive loop by being respectful of her daughter's privacy first, rather than waiting for the daughter to change. This will help the mother feel like she has some influence, even indirectly, on improving the daughter's behavior. More detailed questions about how the rest of the family will react when the mother and daughter are getting along better can be asked, thus extending and creating "the ripple effect" of what the mother initiated.

5. The goal must be stated as the presence rather than the absence of something.

One thing I discovered a long time ago is that everybody knows what the undesirable things are that others do. Others are also quick to point out what you are doing wrong. What is surprising is that such excessive attention to the wrong or undesirable behavior does not seem to help. Some years ago, having tried to lose five pounds, I found myself thinking constantly about what I should not eat. To my dismay, I found I was gaining weight instead of losing it. Once I gave up worrying about what food I should not eat I did quite well. At the time, I did not understand it, but years later I learned that similar phenomenon occurs with problem drinkers (Berg & Miller, 1992). I learned that the more clients told and listened to the "drunk stories" at some AA meetings, the more they found themselves thinking about drinking. On the contrary, many clients reported that the more they concentrated on a healthy life style, the easier it was for them to go with-

out drinking. In looking back, similar mental activities were occurring with my effort to lose weight. It is more useful to keep
one's eyes on the desired goals than to keep thinking about what
one does not want.

Most clients state their goals in terms of the absence of problematic, undesirable behaviors, rather than as the presence of positive
behaviors. Goals such as, "I will not do it again," "I will never get
mad," "He won't steal anymore," "My daughter will stop running
away," "I will never let him in the house when he comes home
drunk," or "I will never slap my child again," are a good start but
are not sufficient. We jokingly call these the "N" words: never,
not, don't, won't, are some examples. Not only is an absence of
problematic behavior difficult to measure and recognize as change
but also some clients do not have any idea of what they will do
instead of leaving the child alone, stealing, fighting, getting mad,
and so on. My experience is that the more detailed the desirable
replacement behavior is, the better, because these replacement
behaviors are clues to the client that she is making progress toward
her goal. The following example shows how the worker can guide
the client toward specifying goals that are described in terms of "I
will make sure my child is supervised by an adult."

Case Example

> Worker: So, when you discipline your child without violence,
> what would you do differently?

> Client: I will just have to not spank him.

> Worker: I can see that it is important to you not to hit him
> again. So what do you suppose you will do instead of
> hitting when you get frustrated?

> Client: Well, I will just walk out, count to ten, send him to his
> room, and then talk to him later.

> Worker: Suppose you do all that, what difference would it
> make in your relationship with your son?

As seen here, the client needs the worker's help in translating her desirable but global idea of "not hitting" her child into concrete, behavioral indicators that will create a change. It is always better to help the client to formulate concrete behaviors that will indicate to her that she is changing. Well-intended but global goals like "I will just not spank him" or "I will do better next time" or "I won't drink any more," are too vague to measure. That is, when the client does *not* hit the child, it is difficult for her to know that she is not hitting. When the client articulates her goals as "I will walk out of the house," "I will send him to his room," "I will count to ten," and so on, the next time she finds herself counting to ten, she can remind herself that she is making progress toward her goal of "not hitting the child." These measurable changes are an outward manifestation of the internal changes that are taking place, therefore, the more detailed and concrete, the better.

Clients often describe their goals in global and vague terms such as, "I will be a good mother," "He will stop lying to me," "We will become a family again," or "She will have a better attitude." The worker's task is to help the client translate these into concrete terms by asking, "When you become a good mother, what will you do that you are not doing right now?" "When your daughter has a better attitude what will she be doing that will let you know that she has a better attitude?" "When you become a family again, what will be going on that will tell you that you are a family again?" Some examples of answers to these questions are: "I will get up in the morning with the kids to cook them breakfast instead of letting them eat dry cereal"; "I will take some time to go to the park with the children"; "I will go to school for conferences"; "My daughter will look me in the eyes when I talk to her instead of looking at the ceiling"; "When we are a family again, maybe we will go to the zoo together, or we will have dinner together sometimes." Having talked about these signs of successes with the worker, the client can recognize her progress toward her goal when these activities occur.

Because it is unrealistic to think that anyone will remember to do all these things in the heat of anger or frustration, the more concrete, detailed options the client has, the better. The process of having to describe these alternatives in a step-by-step fashion forces clients to think out loud, which can help make these ideas more concrete.

6. *The goal must be described as a beginning of new behavior, not an end of undesirable behavior.*

Clients often describe their goals in an idealistic, trouble-free, dream-like way. It can be a positive sign that the client perceives the possibility of life being different from what it is at the moment; however, this kind of goal might take a lifetime to achieve. Therefore, the client needs your assistance to start shaping a goal that is small and concrete. Frequent use of phrases like "starting to feel better," "beginning to have a better attitude," "beginning to be a family," are useful.

Case Example

Let us follow Linda as we try to negotiate a goal. If you remember, Linda decided that having Tish come home first is what made sense to her. Now Linda and the worker need to know what would be the first sign that will tell Linda that Tish is ready to come home.

> Worker: Linda, what would be the first thing that will let you know that Tish is ready to come home?
>
> Linda: She's said it already. I never thought she would say it, but she says she wants to come home.
>
> Worker: So, let us look down the road a bit and think about this. Suppose she comes home first. What would be the first signs that tell you that you and Tish are going to make it so that she will not have to leave home again?
>
> Linda: We will talk together more. She will tell me what's on her mind, what she needs from me, and not run off to my mother's. I will listen to her more. I will remember that

she is a teenager and she has to wear teenager clothes. I
will say this. I never talked to my mother because she
didn't listen to me. I want Tish and me to be different
from my mother and me.

Worker: So, what else will tell you that you and Tish are going
to make it this time?

Linda: I will know how to talk to her nice and not yell at her
like she was my enemy or something.

Worker: So when you do that, what will Tish be doing different that will let you know that you and Tish are different
than you and your mother?

This exchange illustrates how the worker is trying to help Linda
recognize the early signs that she and Tish are starting a new
pattern of interactions that will initiate changes. Not only does
Linda recognize that she is repeating her noncommunicative relationship with Tish, but also she desires to break the repetitive
mother-daughter relationship. As the conversation continues, the
worker can help Linda elaborate on the details of this new relationship in much more concrete and detailed manner.

7. The goal must be viewed as taking a lot of "hard work" by the client.

This point may seem contradictory to you in view of what has
been discussed about the nature of the negotiated goals thus far.
You may wonder how can it be that a small, realistic, and concrete start of some desirable behavior should be thought of as
taking hard work.

In an effort to encourage and motivate the client it is easy for
the worker to make a mistake of saying to the client how simple
and easy it is for her to find a different method of disciplining her
child instead of slapping, kicking, or pushing; how simple it is for
her to "just say no" to her drug and alcohol use. Such an attitude
trivializes the client's own experience of how difficult it is to be
patient with a child who irritates and makes demands on her, day

in and day out, how many times she has tried to leave her abusive partner, how many times she has taken the phone call from school about how her child is causing trouble for other students, and how many different attempts she made to solve her problems.

Even the smallest change may seem like a monumental task when the client is faced with so many conflicting demands. When she is already exhausted, frustrated, and everything seems to go wrong, the last thing the client needs to hear is how simple and easy it will be for her to be nurturing to her child, how she should practice her "active listening," and be realistic about what she can expect from her teenager.

When you emphasize how difficult it is to solve the particular "problem" the client has, you are "blaming" the problem, not the client's lack of effort or lack of intelligence. When you are on the side of the client looking at the "problem" together it seems awesome to handle. This approach not only enhances the team spirit but also acts as a "face saving" device. That is, it is not the client's shortcoming but the enormity and stubbornness of the problem that is the challenge.

In addition, when the client successfully accomplishes the "hard work" she can give herself the credit for this.

8. *What if your goal and the client's goal are different?*

If your view of what is the most urgent problem to solve differs from the client's, you need to establish priorities. Obviously, a child's safety comes first at all times. But when a situation appears chronic, and there is no immediate risk to the child, which is more commonly the case, it may be possible to work first on what the client indicates as goals. The experience of working together successfully on *her* goals is likely to make the client more willing to cooperate around *your* goals.

Even if your goals appear different from those of the client, frequently what the client wants and what you want are the same, only they are expressed differently and with varying degrees of emphasis. For example, the client reluctantly meets with you in order to keep the children with her. Your goal is to insure that the

TREATMENT PLAN

Family Name: _____ Date: _____

Worker's Name: _____

Strengths & Resources:

1.

2.

3.

Successes (Past and Pre-Session):

1.

2.

3.

4.

Goal: (Concrete and Measurable)

1.

2.

3.

Tasks:

Worker:

1.

2.

Client(s):

1.

2.

Comments:

children are safe and reasonably well taken care of, by the biological parent, if possible. The client's goal may be to "stop the social service from coming around," and in order to do that, she must do certain things to meet the minimum standard of adequate child care.

INTERVIEWING AS AN
INTERACTIONAL PROCESS

Professional interviewing is the process of interaction between a client who is seeking service and a professional person who has the knowledge and skills to provide it. Therefore, the worker uses interviewing as a major tool, frequently the only tool, not only to gather information but to direct conversation toward the goal of enhancing the client's sense of competence and self-empowerment.

The client-worker relationship remains a system for the duration of the contract, in which both worker and client influence, and are influenced by, each other. Therefore, when the worker behaves in a certain way, the client will react in certain way, and vice versa (see Chapter 1). This is called the circular interactional process. Over time, this interaction pattern becomes a rule-governed, predictable, repetitive system. The process of interviewing the client to initiate change relies on this pattern of interaction.

Each participant in this interactional system has considerable influence on the ongoing pattern of the relationship, and, at the same time, each is equally dependent on the other to make the system work. Since the purpose of the client-worker system is to benefit the client, it is the worker's task to figure out how to utilize this interactional process to help the client achieve her goals. As you read through the next section, think of yourself as a finely tuned instrument of change for the client. "Use of self" as an instrument means paying attention to the way you phrase the questions, your body posture, your tone of voice, your facial expression, as well as your presentation of yourself as a caring, sincere, and full participant in this journey toward solution-finding.

What to Do, What Not *to Do*

1. Many workers mistake the ventilation of feelings as being a curative tool, and each session or contact becomes a "bitching session." Frequently, just "letting it all hang out" becomes the goal. Others think that "gaining insight through understanding the past brings changes." Just talking about feelings or looking into the past has limited usefulness, since understanding the past will not change the future without action. *Doing* something about their lives change their lives.

It may be necessary to allow the client to vent a certain amount of frustration or anger in order to convey to her that you are interested in her feelings and to acknowledge the difficult life she has had. However, she should not be allowed to "wallow" in how difficult her life has been, or what a lousy childhood she had, and so on, and use it as an excuse for why she cannot change her future and why she cannot be an adequate mother.

2. Whenever possible, direct the conversation to future action, using action-oriented words, such as "So what do you need to *do* so that you feel better about yourself?"

3. Be clear about the client's goal and keep it in mind at all times. Do not allow the client to drift around just to fill the space with words. Each conversation you have with a client has a purpose and should lead in the general direction of finding ways, however small, to achieve her goals.

4. Phrase questions in such a way that the client elaborates on her thinking and her own ideas. Imagine yourself as a client in the following situations and notice the difference in the way you would respond when the question is phrased differently: "Do you know what you have to do so that you don't have to come here anymore?"

When asked this way, the client has the option of saying "Yes" or "No." When this happens, the burden of asking the follow-up question falls to the worker, not the client. It is the client who should take the responsibility for change, not the worker.

You can imagine what kind of questions the therapist will have to come up with to remind the client about what she has to do. Reminder: Whenever you find yourself asking the type of questions that client can respond to with a simple "Yes" or "No" answer, you are already working too hard and the client is not working hard enough. When you find yourself doing this, try questions like the following: "What do you think you need to do so that we can stop meeting like this?" "What do you suppose you have to do so that everybody can stay out of your life?" "What do you suppose your probation officer will have to see you do so they get the idea that you don't have to come here anymore?" "What do you think it will take for you to convince your neighbors that they do not have to call the welfare department?" "What do you think will convince the teacher that you are taking care of your child and that she doesn't have to be concerned about your son?"

Do not be put off or discouraged with a passive response like, "I don't know" accompanied by a shrug of the shoulders. Pretend that you are too slow or dense to understand and re-phrase the question. When the client figures you are not going to be put off easily, she may decide that you passed the first test. If you still get frequent "I don't know" responses, ask the questions from others' perspectives. For example, "What do you suppose your mother will say she will see you do for her to get an idea that she doesn't have to worry about your child?" and so on.

5. Whenever you ask a question, be clear in your mind how the answers to these questions will help direct the client toward thinking about finding solutions.

6. When clients go off on tangents, gently bring them back to the focus of the conversation. For example, "It's still not clear to me, what is it that you have to do so that people will leave you alone?" "I want to come back to this, what will have to be different so that people will not bother you?"

7. It can be useful to deliberately appear "confused" about inconsistencies or gaps in information. Clients are more likely to help a "confused" therapist than an accusatory one. It is not helpful to provoke or anger the client by appearing more

intelligent than the client or by trying to get the client to "admit" her faults. Parroting back to you what she thinks you want to hear is not helpful to this cooperative venture you are trying to build.

8. When you need to confront a client, do not use accusative words or postures. Be sure your tone of voice is not angry or blaming but rather curious, with no preconceived notion of what you want the client to say. Just use a simple, straightforward question like, "So, what do you have to do so that you will not let your boyfriend mistreat your child?"

9. Always keep in mind that it is better to have the client as an ally, not an adversary.

10. Whenever possible use neutral and positive words, and indicate positive movement toward desirable goals as in the following example. "I understand that some people have been very concerned about your family, enough that they asked us to look into your family. How can we help?"

11. Sometimes it is better to assume that the client has asked for help and proceed with that assumption. It helps the client avoid having to ask for help all over again. The client may feel ashamed or humiliated about needing help. Remember, nobody likes to ask for help. Try such approaches as "I understand that you need some help to keep the family together. What do you think is the first thing you need help with?" "It is not hard to see that you need some help with keeping your family together. What is the first thing you have to do so that your family can stay together?"

These approaches help the client and the worker to move right into the task of figuring out goals. They allow some, not all, clients to have some room to "save face." Some people are too proud to ask for help, or too embarrassed that someone found out they are not doing an adequate job with their children. We need to be sensitive to such common human emotions.

6

Useful Questions and Other Interviewing Techniques

THE WORKER'S DECISION TO ask certain questions and not others may appear haphazard and random to the uninitiated. But each professional transaction between the worker and the client is a purposeful one. Thus, *which* questions the worker decides to ask, and *how, when, whom* to ask, has significant impact on the client-worker relationship. At times, not asking certain questions within a certain context has a powerful impact on the client. Focusing on certain aspects of the client's life while ignoring others conveys certain messages and impressions to the client within the context of this professional relationship.

For example, when the worker asks a detailed question about a client's childhood experience of being physically abused by his mother, certain messages are conveyed to the client, most significantly that the worker views the client's history of abuse as an important link to his current abusive behavior of his children. On the other hand, when the same worker asks the same client detailed information about how he managed to be so loving to his own child, it implies something else, that is, that the worker is more interested in finding solutions than in fixing blame. The decision to ask certain questions and not others must always be related to what the goals are.

Some years ago I asked a wise successful salesman of farming products about his sales approach. He described how he visited each farmer on his rounds of his sales territory. Even though he made a good living by selling farm supplies and products, animal feeds, fertilizers, seeds, and so on, he never mentioned the products he was selling. Instead, he would visit with each farmer and talk about his children, family members, the weather, crop and cattle conditions, and so on. Given the context of his sales job and the nature of his visits, his no-pressure sales strategy is much more powerful and effective than if he made a high-pressure sales pitch.

Since the interview is the single most important tool the worker has, the topic merits our close attention. We need to look at *what* to ask, *when, how, whom* to ask, and for *what* purpose. What the worker decides to find out from the client should be related to what the worker views as the goal of his professional relationship with the client. As you have seen in this book so far, all of these questions follow two different tracks, that is, the client's perceptions about his situation and the client's perception of other's perception of him. We call these individual and relationship questions. As you will see, the relationship questions provide us with some valuable data on the client's social and contextual situation. Because FBS clients are related to many other social service systems, such as schools, health care, criminal justice, legal, and other systems, it is imperative that the worker is informed of the client's perception of these other helping relationships. This chapter describes and discusses ways to use the "five useful questions" in FBS. They are questions about: past successes, exceptions, miracles, scales, and coping strategies.

PAST SUCCESSES AND
PRE-SESSION CHANGE

Through the interviewing process, the worker can focus on the client's past successes, that is, when he was functioning well enough not to require social service interventions. It is empowering for the client to realize that there was a period in his life when he was more successful than he feels at the moment. He needs help to remember these successful periods, because it is easy to forget this competent functioning while under the stress of dealing with current problems. Once the forgotten problem-solving skills are uncovered, the next task for the worker and the client is to find ways to adapt these skills to his current difficulties.

This section will discuss and list examples of questions that elicit helpful information and ways to make use of the client's past and current successes. For example, imagine asking a client the following questions:

- "The record indicates that two years ago you had your child returned to you from the foster home. What did you do right that time?"
- "What do you suppose the social worker thinks you did to convince him that you were ready to have your child returned?"

Compare those questions with these:

- "The record indicates that the Department placed your child in a foster home. Do you remember why that happened?"
- "What do you suppose the social worker thought was wrong with your parenting that made it necessary to take your child away from you?"

It is not difficult to see the difference between the first set of questions and the second set. The first set acknowledges in a matter of fact fashion, not only past problems, but also past successes. There is a less blaming tone to the interaction; this is displayed by the phrasing of the statement: " . . . you had your child returned . . . ," which possesses more positive connotations than the equally true statement, " . . . the Department placed your child in a foster home."

Another disadvantage to the way the second set of questions is posed is that questions related to "why" usually imply judgment: When we ask "why" something bad has happened, we are actually asking, "whom can be blamed?" It is clear to clients that the question is rhetorical — *they* are to blame, otherwise they would not be involved with social services. Sometimes it is more powerful not to ask the obvious questions when it is clear why the worker is there. These are small but significant differences that makes a great difference when dealing with the FBS clients.

When asked about their past successes or the times when they felt positively about themselves, clients frequently become briefly disoriented and appear startled. Many clients report that this is the first time they have been treated as having a brain or as having done some things right in their past. In fact, many clients become tearful and then calmer and more cooperative — often their expression and posture changes. It is easier for clients to become hopeful about themselves when they can look back at past successes. The following are some examples of questions that the worker can ask.

- "How did you manage to get out of that abusive relationship with Tyler? How did you find enough strength to get rid of him?"
- "It is not easy to raise three children on your own. How did you do it?"
- "After having been through what you've been through, how did you find enough strength to keep pushing on?"
- "What do you suppose you need to do so that you'll feel good about yourself and in control of your life again?"
- "What would it take for you to bring back the confidence you had when you were in high school?"
- "What do you suppose your mother would say you need to do to bring back your old self-confidence?"

Or consider this interaction:

Worker: How do you manage to force yourself to get up in the morning?

Client: It's only because I don't want my kids to drop out of school like I did.

Worker: You really want your children to do better than you have done. You must love them very much.

Client: They are all I have. I want them to get through school, get good jobs, have good things I can't have.

Worker: What are you doing so that you can continue to hope
and to try one more time? What do you think your mother
would say keeps you going?

These are some examples of how you can help clients regain
self-confidence and help them realize that they still have the ability to shape their lives in the way they want them to be. So, now
that you helped the client discover his past successes, what next?
Since he has experienced successes in the past you can (a) remind
the client about his past, and (b) ask him what it will take to
repeat these successes. Such questions should focus on what he will
need to do in order to use his past skills in the current situation.
Even if the client's social and personal situation has changed a
great deal (for example, he is now divorced, his grandmother has
died), you can still discuss ways that can adapt old coping strategies to a new situation.

All of the above questions can be phrased in such a way that
the client can be encouraged to be a detached observor of himself,
and thus make rational, long-term decisions that are not based on
impulsive and emotional reactions.

Since the client and worker first meet because of a problem, it
is all too easy to focus only on the difficulty and to miss the fact
that the client is likely to have already done things to diminish the
problem, even if only a little bit. In fact, research (Weiner-Davis,
de Shazer, & Gingerich, 1987) shows that clients describe pre-
session changes in at least two-thirds of cases. Pre-session changes
are those changes that the client made toward the goals between
the time he set up an appointment and the first meeting with the
therapist. My own clinical experience bears this out, even if the
period between the phone call and the first session is as little as 24
hours. During the first meeting with the client, FBS workers can
ask what positive things have occurred between the time the appointment was made and the first home visit. If these changes are
in the same direction as what he was hoping to accomplish through
the services FBS offers, it is even better. Such initial change, however small or insignificant it seems, that the client generates on

his own is the natural product of his way of finding solutions to his problem. The worker's task is to support, enhance, and amplify the initial start-up of positive changes, however small. My enthusiasm for such pre-session change stems from the recognition that the client has generated movement toward how he wants his life to be and therefore he needs the worker's full endorsement and support to continue. More importantly, the solutions emerge from within the client's personal or family system, which suggests that there is a natural fit between the problem and the solution.

Case Example

Sharon, age 21, has two children, ages 14 months and five years; she is expecting her third child in about a month. Her relationship with her boyfriend, Archie, has been a turbulent, "on and off" one for the past three years. Archie's problems with job instability, drinking, drug use, and fighting led to frequent physical abuse of Sharon.

Sharon had a rocky relationship with her divorced parents, with whom she had fought since her early teens. She said they had always been critical of her parenting, her choice of relationships with men, and numerous other issues. Sharon reported that her mother had "nothing good" to say about her and that her father said it was her fault that Archie mistreated her and pushed her around when he was drunk. Of course, Sharon had given them her share of grief: she started to run away at 13, played truant from school, flirted with drinking and drug use, became pregnant at 15, and eventually dropped out of school. She and her first child had lived in a foster home because her parents refused to take them home from the hospital. She and Archie tried living together for a while but could not afford the housing. Sharon and Archie were currently living with their respective parents but act as if they are "married."

Sharon came to the attention of the FBS because her four-year-old daughter was caught in their most recent fight and sustained a minor injury. Between the run to the hospital, meeting with the CPS worker, and getting ready for the imminent delivery of her baby, Sharon decided that she and the children deserved something better than what they had been getting from Archie, and she announced that she was through with him.

So, what was different this time? What made her think that she would follow through with her decision to break up with Archie? After all, she had done this off and on for three years, and she would soon have Archie's third child.

Sharon listed several different things she did the day before her first appointment with the worker, all things she has never done before. She told Archie's mother off. She said it was pretty scary and took a lot of guts because Archie's mother was a "powerful lady" who screamed at her about her "selfishness" and the grandparent's right to see her grandchildren and threatened her with a court action to assert her rights.

She called the hospital where she planned to deliver her baby and arranged to have the baby placed in a special area that would allow only limited viewing to a special list of visitors. She calmly announced to Archie that their relationship was over and hung up on him when he started to cry and beg her to take him back. Sharon made an arrangement with friends to stay in phone contact in case she weakened and was tempted to take Archie back. She said this was the first time she felt angry at him for his refusing to take responsibility for her and the children. This was really a first. She had usually felt hurt in the past and suffered quietly or at other times extracted remorse and a promise to do better in the future from Archie.

The worker decided to utilize her pre-session change and complimented and supported her decision to make a new life for herself and the children. The worker kept wondering what was different about yesterday that had given her the strength to make all these changes. At first, Sharon said she was not clear about what made the difference, but later began to form the opinion that the new baby on the way made the difference. She felt that her three children needed responsible adults and more stability in their lives, and she realized that no matter how much she fought with Archie, he was not going to become responsible.

Since Sharon was so strong about her decision to remain separated from Archie, it was suggested that she "keep track of what you do when you overcome the urge either to ask him to come back or to take him back when he begs."

Sharon was beaming when the worker met her the following session. She went over all her meetings with Archie and reported that, although tempted many times to go back to the old ways, she had handled things differently, which made Archie mad. Many things she did were new for her, such as going out with girlfriends, contacting old friends, making decisions independently of Archie, and telling him that he could not just come over on the spur of the moment.

She provided a good example of how she was handling things differently. Archie called and begged her to allow him to visit the children. Sharon said firmly that since he had not showed up for three weeks she was not going to allow him to "waltz in and out of their lives." He had to show her that he was committed to his children by demonstrating his ability to stick to regular visitation hours. He agreed to this and now comes only at the visitation hours to pick up the children, giving her a much needed break from them. This was clearly just a beginning but it was an important one to build on.

EXCEPTION FINDING QUESTIONS

"Exceptions" (see Chapter 1 for details) are times when the problem could have happened but did not. The worker and the client need to examine *who* did *what, when, where,* and *how* so that the problem did not happen, in other words, how the patterns around the problems were changed. Such interruptions, however small, lead to more significant changes.

Case Example

Every time six-year-old Tyrone would start fighting, hitting his sister, Michelle, and making himself a nuisance, his grandmother would grab him, pull him away, and scold him. He would then throw a tantrum, crying, kicking, and holding his breath. One day the grandmother decided she was too tired to intervene and left Tyrone and Michelle alone to fight it out. To her surprise,

Tyrone started playing with Michelle, who ignored his usual invitation for a fight.

In this example, there are several exceptions to the usual interaction sequence: Grandmother's decision not to intervene in the fight, Michelle's spontaneous decision to ignore Tyrone's invitation to fight; and Tyrone's doing something other than what he normally does (i.e., playing with his sister). If all three people who are involved in this exception were to repeat this scenario, either together or separately, there is a good chance that they will have much more peaceful times when they are together.

When Problems Occur in Limited Context

Frequently, problematic behaviors happen only within certain physical, relational, or social contexts. For example, Jamie loses his temper only at home and not at other places, such as at school, at church, or when at his aunt's house. Jena becomes unmanageable only with mother and not with mother's new boyfriend or with a baby-sitter. Joe loses his temper and becomes violent only when he has been drinking quite a bit or when he discusses money with his wife. It is important to find out in detail what happens when the person does not have a problem, since the client can learn to transfer the abilities he uses successfully in one setting to another situation. Clients often describe how a husband, for example, is so different when he is with his friends, coworkers, or boss that these other people would never guess what he is like at home. It would be productive to find out what is different about those situations that cause him to behave so differently, since this may give clues about changing his behavior at home.

For example, the police were called to take Beverly to the county hospital. She had "gone on a rampage" and "trashed the house" when she got into a fight with her husband. She readily agreed that she had "just lost it" and really could not afford to keep doing so. Beverly acknowledged that since she was a child she had had a hot temper. In the process of looking for exceptions to her "hot temper" it was learned that she had held a job at the warehouse of a large grocery store chain for three years and that she "loved working there." She was considered a good employee and had never lost her temper with her supervisor or coworkers, even though they were "rowdy, condescending, macho guys" who teased her for being a woman. Looking at this as an exception, the worker and Beverly found many ways she managed to control her temper and "keep her cool," even when she could have easily lost her temper with her coworkers. Raising these questions forced Beverly to think of herself differently than she had before; she could be calm, responsible, and handle her temper under stress. She had to modify her view of herself.

In another example, 17-year-old Michael was described as a hostile, aggressive young man with poor impulse control. He cut school, flunked most classes year after year, and was unmanageable at home and in the community. He had a long list of problematic and delinquent behaviors, such as running away, truancy, stealing, breaking and entering, and using and dealing drugs. Many attempts to solve his problems through various treatments had failed. After holding up an old woman, Michael finally ended up in a correctional institution where he became a model student, worked in the cafeteria, participated in sports activities, and earned privileges for weekend furlough after four months, which was considered amazing, given his destructive past behaviors. When the worker spent a great deal of time with Michael asking questions, with genuine curiosity, about how he was able to change so drastically, he had various explanations. Even though his answers to these questions were usually related to his confinement to the corrections facility, the worker became even more curious about his success, considering how other boys in the same facility did not fare as well as he did.

After a considerable amount of time spent thinking it over Michael finally came to realize that he really did not want to repeat his past and that it had its downsides. After examining these downsides, Michael eventually decided that he was beginning to like this new side of himself, which was a new experience for him.

Giving recognition for successful periods in a client's life and acknowledging his ability to function in competent fashion, even in limited areas, helps the client get started in the right direction. The next task for the worker is to encourage the client to maintain and increase the number of areas in which he is successful.

Ways to Ask Questions

The following are examples of questions designed to help a client discover his own strengths and abilities to solve problems. Even when the success may be very small compared to the numerous problems the client faces, solutions start with small steps.

It is always better for the client to come up with his own solutions rather than being told what to do. When it is his own idea, he is more likely to be committed to successful solutions. In addition, if a solution is generated from within the client's existing resources, it fits naturally with his way of doing things, and is easier to do more of. Furthermore, these solutions are likely to be more congruent with his life style than any newly learned behavior, and he is less likely to relapse.

Worker: I can see that you have every reason to be depressed. So when do you suppose you get a little bit less depressed?

Client: Well, I'm not sure. I get depressed all the time. I feel a little bit better when I have some money to spend on my kids. I feel like I am a better mother when I can buy things for my kids.

Worker: So, what would you say is different with you when you can buy things for your children?

Client: Well, then I feel like I'm a good mother. I hate being poor because it reminds me of my own mistakes. I feel worse at the end of the month when I run out of money.

Worker: So how would you say you are different when you are a little bit less depressed?

Client: Well, I force myself to get up in the morning even when I don't feel like it, get the kids ready for school, maybe even get a little bit more cheerful when I force myself. Maybe even walk to school with the kids, and even get out of the house. Then I can forget how depressing my life is.

Worker: So, when you force yourself to get out of bed, walk

the kids to school, and so on, what do you suppose your children will notice different about you?

Client: I try not to show them how depressed I am but I suppose they know. Sometimes when I don't get out of bed in the morning, the children fight more. I guess they want to see me happier because it makes them calmer.

Worker: So, what would it take you to force yourself to get up in the morning more often?

As you can see from the exchange, the worker ignored some issues that the client has no control over at the moment, such as not having money, previous mistakes, being depressed. Instead, he concentrates on her current small but useful successes. When the client forces herself to get up in the morning, things generally turn out little better. Clearly, the client needs to repeat this, and the last question the worker asks in this exchange forces the client to think about what she needs to do more of.

Worker: You are saying that you didn't drink for five days last week. How did you do it? I am amazed that you controlled your drinking for five days. How did you do it?

Client: It's only five days. I've gone longer than that when I was pregnant.

Worker: You did? How did you do that? Wasn't it hard? You mean you did it all alone without going into treatment? How long did you not drink at that time?

Client: Well, I didn't want to hurt my baby when I was pregnant. It was hard at first but I just told myself I'm not going to do it. So, when I'd go out, I used to drink soda.

Worker: That's amazing. You must be a strong person. Now, tell me how you didn't drink for five days this time.

Client: I didn't have any money. I was broke.

Worker: Come on, I know that if you really wanted to drink, you would have found ways to get that drink. How did you manage not to drink?

Later in the session the following questions can be asked:

- "Tell me, what is different for you at those times when you do not drink?"
- "How do you explain to yourself that the problem doesn't happen at those times?"
- "Where did you get the idea to do it that way?"
- "What do you suppose your mother would say you do different when you do not drink?"
- "What will have to happen for you to do it more often?"
- "What else would you say you do differently when the problem doesn't happen?"
- "What would you and your girlfriend do differently when the problem doesn't happen?"

These questions should be followed up with questions that reinforce the idea of success:

- "So, what do you have to do so that you can continue to say "No" to drinking?"
- "What do you suppose you and your girlfriend will be doing different instead of drinking (getting depressed, etc.)?"
- "If your girlfriend were here and if I were to ask her, what do you suppose she would say she notices different about you when you do not get depressed (drink, act angry, etc.)?"
- "What would she say has to happen for that to happen more often?"
- "How long would she say this has to continue for her to get an idea that your problem is solved?"
- "When the problem is solved, how do you think your relationship with your sister (mother, friend, etc.) would change? What will you be doing then that you are not doing now?"

As you can see, the worker here is trying very hard to give the client credit for his own success while getting him to realize that it is something he *did* rather than something he allowed to happen to him.

In the process of having to explain his actions to the worker, it becomes more and more clear to the client that he did something to create an exception to the problem. In this way, he can own up to his success. It is then easier for him to own up to his failures when they are placed within a larger context that includes success. The worker's task is to ask questions about exceptions whenever the client reports failures, mistakes, or problems. The next task for the worker is to find ways to reinforce the client's success and amplify it by increasing his self-confidence and self-esteem.

MIRACLE QUESTIONS

In the close to ten years since the team at the Brief Family Therapy Center in Milwaukee began asking this question (Berg, 1988; de Shazer, 1985), hundreds of therapists and workers around the world have used this strange question with remarkable results. The miracle question literally asks clients to disregard their current troubles for a moment and imagine what their lives will be like in a successful future. Getting the client to imagine that "a miracle has happened and your problem is solved" has a powerful clinical impact. First, it creates a vivid image or vision of what his life will be like when the problem is solved, and second, he can see some hope for himself that life can be different. It creates a personal possible self, which is not modelled after someone else's ideas of what his life should be like.

The question goes like this: "Suppose one night there is a miracle while you are sleeping and the problem that brought you to the attention of the FBS is solved. Since you are sleeping, you don't know that a miracle has happened or that your problem is solved. What do you suppose you will notice different the next morning that will tell you that the problem is solved?"

Having experimented with a number of different ways to ask this question over the years, we discovered that the following elements must be addressed in order to maximize the effectiveness of this question. They are:

- suppose [sets the stage for imagination]
- miracle happened [sets the tone as one of playfulness]
- the problem is solved [for the moment, the "how" of solution is deemphasized]
- you don't know (because you are sleeping) [again, empha-

sizes the future: a problem that is solved, rather than a problem
that needs to be solved]
- what will be different to indicate that [focuses on details]
- miracle happened and the problem is solved? [future focus]

Client reactions vary. Some clients start to sit up straight, and
to describe in detail how their lives will be transformed. Some
clients are genuinely surprised at their own words of hope. Some
listen attentively to family members' descriptions of miracles for
themselves as well as for others.

Occasionally, clients talk about winning a lottery, or other "pie
in the sky" dreams. When these dreams are handled with humor,
clients usually settle down and become much more realistic. They
begin to describe how their lives will change in concrete, specific,
small, achievable terms. It is useful to help the client describe the
imagined changes in as much detail as possible. The first therapeutic task is to elicit this information in such a way that the
client can see the possibility of his "miracle" really happening.
The next task is to help the client figure out what steps he might
take to initiate those behaviors that will lead to "miracles." The
more detailed these descriptions the better, since the more possibilities the client lists, the more likely it is that he will be able to
perform at least few of those as immediately as "tomorrow morning." There are other variations on this question, for example,
Dolan (1991) asks a sexual abuse survivor to imagine becoming a
wise old woman someday and to imagine what kind of advice she
would give to her younger self. The following dialogue offers an
example of the miracle question:

Client: I will have a job, have a nice place to live, nice clothes,
will have a man who cares about me, not just uses me,
but really cares about me. My children will be happy,
they will do well in school. Maybe I will be in school so
that I will get training to get a job.

Worker: Well, that sounds like the end of a big miracle. What
do you suppose is the first thing—in the morning—that
will tell you that, "Hey, something is different in my life?"

Client: Well, I will get up earlier, have some time for myself, say good morning to the kids with a smile, get them up, sit down with them for breakfast, tell them to have a good day, and send them off to school.

Worker: If you were to pretend that the miracle has happened, what would be the first thing you would do? [This is a strong suggestion that the client has to *do* something to solve the problem.]

Here are more examples of follow-up questions:

• What would it take to pretend that this miracle has happened? Anything else? What else?
• If you were to do that, what will be the first change you will notice about yourself?
• Who would be the first person to notice the next day that something is different about you after the miracle?
• What would your mother (husband, friend, sister, etc.) notice different about you, if you didn't tell her that there's been a miracle? What else? Anything else?
• What would your mother (or others) do different then?
• What do you think will be different between you and your mother then?
• If you were to take these steps, what would you notice different around your house?
• If you were to do that, what would be the first thing your children will notice different around your house? [Again, a strong suggestion that the client can do something.]
• What would they do different then? What else? Anything else?

You may have noticed that these examples use proactive words and phrases such as "do" and "take these steps" quite frequently. It is very purposely designed to suggest that (a) the client has to *do* things "differently" in order to bring about changes in his life; (b) that *HE* is the one who has to do them; and (c) that he has to take an active role in shaping his life by working out his own ideas of a useful solution. Answering these miracle questions will provide him with clues on what first steps he needs to take to find solutions and will show him how his life *will* change, thus giving him hope that his life *can* change. Regardless of whether a client imagines that the miracle happens through a force outside of herself, such as divine intervention, or through her conscious effort — as this mother describes how she will be different with her children the next morning — this miracle question seems to separate the problems from solutions to them. There occurs a disconnection between the problem and solution.

Miracles Involving Others in the Family?

During my frequent workshop presentations and teaching seminars, many FBS workers raise questions about clients whose answers to miracle questions have to do with others changing. For example, a mother's answer to a miracle question is that her uncontrollable teenage son will transform into a perfect child. Since this mother's waiting for her son to change not only will take years, if it ever happens at all, but also will leave her feeling helpless and out of control of her life; you need to help this mother focus on what *she can do* immediately. The following are some examples of how you can help the mother redirect her attention to what she can do while waiting for her son to come to his senses.

> Client: My son will get up on his own, get ready for school without my yelling at him to get up, get his homework ready, and get out the door on time for the school bus. Most of all, he will stay in school all day instead of skipping out. I won't get a phone call from school telling me that I have to come and get him.

> Worker: That's a lot, and I guess it will take a while for that to happen. Let's just suppose that happens. What do you suppose he will say how you will be different when he can do all this?

> Client: He will probably say that I will be nice to him, talk

softly to him, let him do things, like let him off the ground-
ing, maybe even get back to talking to each other.

Worker: Suppose you were to do all these. What do you think
he will say how he will be different?

Client: He will say it will be easier for him to be a part of the
family. He sure doesn't feel much like a part of a family
right now because I am always yelling at him. I am sure
he doesn't like that. We weren't like that before.

Worker: So, what has to come first; does he have to change
first, then you will be nicer to him or do you have to be
nicer to him before he will change?

Client: Now that you put it that way, I guess I can start being
nicer first.

Worker: What is the small thing you can do to let him know
that you are being nicer to him?

Occasionally clients come up with solutions that are beyond all
realistic possibilities. For example, a very angry teenager thought
that all her troubles would be solved if her single-parent mother
"dropped dead"; an unrealistic adolescent answered that all his
troubles would be over if only he could move out on his own.
Clearly, not a very realistic idea; yet, if you remind him of that,
he will brush you aside as being "like everybody else." Instead of
giving gentle reminders that his idea will not work, you might use
the following approach.

Worker: Well, I don't think it will happen. But let's just suppose for the sake of discussion it does happen. Just suppose
your parents "drop dead" and your problem is solved.
What will you be doing then that you are not doing right
now? What difference would it make for you?

Client: I will be in my own apartment, going to school, maybe
even to work, having peace and quiet. I will get along

with people. I will have a job, money in my pocket, won't be fighting with my mom.

Worker: What will your friends say how you will be different then?

Client: They will say I won't be so angry; calmer, yeah, calmer and nice to people.

As is clear from these examples, when the worker accepts the client's false premise that everything in life will turn out fine "if only" the unrealistic happens, the client often is able still to carry out the scenario to its logical conclusion and the solution usually returns to what *he* will do differently.

Miracle Questions for Goal-Setting Purpose

Depending on how the worker phrases the questions, the answers to miracle questions can be useful for guiding the client in the general direction of desired change. When the picture of the miracle (solution) is similar to what the client wants from his contact with you, it is easy to discern in which direction you need to move (see Chapter 5 on goal setting).

SCALING QUESTIONS

Scaling questions are very versatile. Because they are simple, we find that even children old enough to understand number concepts (that 10 is greater than 5, for example), respond very well. Adults whose thinking style tends to be concrete, precise, and pragmatic also respond very well. Scaling is simple to keep track of and does not require the sophisticated intellectual ability to think abstractly in order to respond.

As you will notice, scaling questions can be used to assess self-esteem, pre-session change, self-confidence, investment in change, willingness to work hard to bring about desired changes, prioritizing of problems to be solved, perception of hopefulness, and evaluation of progress, and so on — things usually are considered too abstract to quantitate. It also helps the client to assess what his significant others think about these situations.

This question has a wide application. The more you experiment with it, the more proficient you will become at using it. Experiment and play with it. One word of caution: You may have to specify time limits, such as "today," "last week," "during the past month."

The following are some practical examples of how these scaling questions can be put to use. Notice the careful wording that conveys hope, action, and changes in small steps.

Worker: On a scale of 1 to 10, with 10 meaning you have every confidence that this problem can be solved, and 1 means no confidence at all, where would you put yourself today?

Client: I would say 5, in the middle.

Worker: If I were to ask your boyfriend where he thinks you are on the same scale, what do you suppose he would say?

Client: He would probably say higher, like maybe 7 or 8, even.

Worker: What do you suppose he would say is the reason he is so much more confident about your solving this problem?

Client: He is always backing me up. He always tells me that I can do it, only if I put my mind to it. He doesn't know how hard it is to have such confidence.

Worker: On the same scale, how hopeful are you that this problem can be solved?

Client: I would say 6.

Worker: What would be different in your life when you move up just one step, from 6 to 7?

Client: I would be less upset with myself. For a change, I will actually say no to my mother. My mother runs my life and I will say to her to leave me alone and not tell me what to do all the time.

Worker: If your boyfriend were here and I were to ask him what he thinks it will take you to go up from 6 to 7, what would he say?

Client: I'm not sure but I would guess that he will say I have to stand up to my mother.

Worker: Do you agree with him on that?

Client: Yeh, he is right about that. I have to be strong with my mother. She is a powerful lady, though.

Worker: What do you suppose he would say what it will take you to stand up to your mother?

Client: He will say I have to stop drinking first.

Worker: So, how interested are you in wanting to stop drinking?

Client: I have to stop drinking. It's killing me, I know I have to do it.

Worker: So, what is the first thing you have to do to stop drinking?

Client: I just have to stop drinking when I get upset with my mother.

Worker: What do you suppose your boyfriend would say is the first step for you to stop drinking?

Here, the worker is using the scaling numbers to gather information not only about what will give the client more hope about herself, but also about how much support the client is getting from her environment. The next step is to help the client to talk about the steps she needs to take toward solving the problem. The more the client is encouraged to say what she has to do, and needs to do, the more she believes it is her idea to stop drinking. Repetition of the same question in several different ways is a good way to reinforce and support client decisions. The more the client repeats an idea, the easier it is for the client to own the solutions because she will convince herself that it is her idea, and not yours.

Motivation

Following are questions that encourage the client to explore his motivation to change:

- "On the same scale, how much would you say you are willing to work to solve this problem?"
- "What do you suppose your mother (or some significant other) would say?"
- "Where would you put your husband on the same scale?" (The closer to 10 the client is, the more invested she is.)

When a client gives a low number on the same scale, it can be followed up with:

- "What do you suppose they would say you need to do to move up 1 point on the same scale?"
- "What do you suppose they would say they need to see you do for them to get the idea that you are at 6?"
- "What would it take you to move up from 5 to 6?" or "When you move from 5 to 6, what would you be doing that you are not doing now?"
- "When you move from 5 to 6, what would others notice different about you that they don't notice now? What do you suppose you will notice different about them then?"
- "How invested would your wife say she is, on the same scale, in helping you solve this problem?"
- "How do you explain that she is more interested in your changing than you are? What do you suppose she would say is the reason that she is so interested in your moving from 5 to 6?"

Asking these questions helps the client become more aware of his current position, where he wants to get to, what he is doing that helps, what he will need to do, and how the people around him might notice differences and respond differently as he changes, thus enabling him to make an informed decision on what step he needs to take.

Self-Esteem

Worker: Let's say 100 means you have become the ideal kind
of person you always wanted to be, how close would you
say you are to being 100 today?

Client: I would say 35. I am not feeling too hot today.

Worker: On the same scale, what would you say was the clos-
est to being 100 you ever came?

Client: I would say 70. That was two years ago.

Worker: What was going on in your life then?

Client: I was more confident about myself then. I was going
to school, felt good about myself, I had hope and I knew
I could do it.

Worker: What would it take for you to move closer to 70?

Client: I know what I have to do. I just have to do it. God, it's
like it was 100 years ago but it was only two years ago. I
was a good student, I had ambition. I could see where I
was going.

Worker: So, what do you have to do to move up from 35 to
40?

Client: That's easy. I just have to get up everyday at the same
time and force myself to go look for a job.

Worker: So, when you get up at the same time and force yourself to look for a job, what do you suppose you will notice
different about yourself?

The worker does not have to know details of the client's past or
the content of his problem in order to help him figure out what
he has to do. The client has a clear sense of what he needs to do to
get himself moving on the right path.

The last question the worker asked forced the client to imagine
how he would be different when he actually does what he knows
he has to do. This is a powerful motivator, particularly when

he can see what lies beyond the hard work of making necessary changes.

The following are more examples on the same theme, which can be used to help motivate the client.

> Worker: Let's say 10 means the best you have felt about yourself, and 1 means the worst, what is the highest you ever felt about yourself?
>
> Client: I would say 7.
>
> Worker: What were you doing different at the time? (What was going on in your life at the time? What do you suppose your mother would say she noticed different about you in those days?)

Whatever the client's answers are, the worker can usually find ways to encourage the client to take steps toward repeating the 7 again. Even if the client is not ready to take steps to move back to 7 again at this time, at least he has a chance to review the successful period in his life and remember all the good things he did to arrive at 7. Since this is something he did one time, the potential for him to repeat this is already there. This is an example of utilizing past successes.

Assessment of Progress

Scaling questions can also be used to assess the client's perception of the progress he is making with the FBS program. The following examples show a number of different ways this question can be applied.

- "Let's say 10 is where you want your life to be and 1 is where we started our work together, where would say you are at today?"
- "Where do you suppose your mother would say you are?"
- "What has to be different in your life for you to say that you are 1 point higher?"
- "What would it take you to move it up 1 point?"

- "What do you suppose your mother will say you need to do to move up 1 point?"
- "When you move up 1 point, who would be the first to notice the change?"
- "When you move up 1 point, what would he notice different about you that he doesn't see now?"
- "When your mother notices these differences in you, what do you suppose she will do differently with you?"
- "When that happens, what will you do to let her know that you like what she is doing?"
- "What do you suppose she will do then?"
- "At what point do you think you will say we don't have to meet like this?"
- "When things are at 7 or 8, what will be different with you that will tell you that you can go on with your life without outside help?"

Case Example

The following is an example of the treatment of a family whose presenting problem centered on 12-year-old Timmy.

Worker: What do think you will notice different when Timmy moves up from 6 to 7?

Client: I will be able to trust him enough to take him to a shopping mall without getting worried about him stealing things.

Worker: When you can do that, what else would you notice different about him that will tell you that it's OK to take him to a shopping mall?

Client: Well, he will come home on time, not fight with his brother, clean his room, take care of the dog mess in the yard, and not get phone calls from the teacher everyday.

Worker: That sounds more like 8 or 9 than 7 to me.

Client: I guess you are right. I promised to take him fishing when he gets to be 8 or 9.

Worker: So, given what you've seen Timmy do so far since we started our work together, how confident are you that you can take him fishing?

Client: Getting pretty close; I would say maybe another week or so.

These are some examples of questions the worker can ask to assess what the client's perceptions are about his own or someone else's progress in treatment. The case example described above provides good ideas of how to help a parent develop more realistic expectations for a child's behavior without lecturing.

Assessment of Relationship

- "On the same scale, how much would she say she wants this marriage (or relationship)?" "How much would she say *you* want this marriage?"
- "How much would you say you want this marriage to work out? How much do you think *she* wants to work on this marriage?"
- "How do you explain that you want this marriage more than she does?"
- "What do you know about this marriage that she doesn't know, that makes you more invested in this marriage?"

The same can be asked about the absent partner's perception by asking questions in the following manner:

- "What would she say she knows about this marriage that you don't know that makes her so realistic (or optimistic or pessimistic, depending on situation)?"
- "From her point of view, what do you suppose she would say it will take her to want this marriage as much as you do? What else?"

As you can see, the value of scaling questions is limitless. It allows you to find out about all kinds of vague concepts or ideas that clients cannot explain. These questions help make things more concrete, and thus change and progress are easier to notice and measure.

Application with Children

My clinical experience is that children as young as seven or eight years old can easily use scaling questions. It is more helpful, however, to use a visual scale, using a blackboard, or writing pad and draw a graphic scale (this can be a simple number line). You might want to explore their perceptions by using the width of your arms as a measure; use the floor as 1 or the lowest point and raise your hand up in the air to indicate higher points.

Case Example

Eight-year-old Melissa, a bright and delightful child, was brought to therapy because she had been molested in a shopping mall. After several sessions, she was making good progress. During the fifth session, the therapist decided to ask her, using scaling questions, how much progress she thought she was making in therapy. It was explained to Melissa that 10 meant her life would go back to normal like before the incident and 1 meant where she was when she first started to come to see the therapist. Drawing a line from left to right across a writing board, the worker asked where she thought she was on the line. She indicated her progress to be about 7.

> Worker: What do you suppose it will take you to go from here to there? (*indicating point 10*)
> (*Melissa thought for a long time, shifting her weight from one leg to the other.*)
>
> Melissa: I know what.
>
> Worker: What?
>
> Melissa: I will burn the clothes I was wearing when it happened.
>
> Worker: What a wonderful idea! Melissa, I think that's exactly the right thing to do.

The worker suggested to the mother that they devise a ritual around the burning of the clothes as a family, followed by a celebration, such as going out to a fancy restaurant. The case terminated.*

Working with Young Children

One of the benefits of presenting and conducting workshops on FBS is that I meet a number of very creative, innovative, and talented therapists and workers from around the world. One such person, Paul Shaw, from Dayton, Ohio, devised an adaptation of this scaling question in working with small children. He was generous enough to allow me to write about it and describe it to other workers who work with children. He devised a scale using faces that change gradually from frowning to smiling. The child can indicate where she is on the scale, without having to have a grasp on numbers.

Others have devised line graphs to chart the progress the child is making by tracking his progress. Young and adolescent clients delight in tracing and monitoring their own progress, and it is easy to see how this will be a valuable aid in internalizing their observations and assessments.

COPING QUESTIONS

Every once in a while, FBS workers run into situations where a client has experienced extreme deprivation or has a personal history that includes severe abuse or mental illness. As a result, workers can feel utterly hopeless about the client's future. When faced with such a situation, the most common reaction is to reassure the depressed and hopeless person by saying things like, "Everything will turn out all right," "Don't worry, look at the positive side," "You have so much going for you, look at yourself." The most frustrating aspect of such efforts is that the client is *not* reassured; if anything, he becomes more hopeless, and often utters even more desperate things. As you may have learned by now, self-esteem and self-assurance are not qualities that a person takes in from

*Karen Jick was the therapist in this case.

external sources but are generated from within. Pep talks and exhortations are short-lived. What stays with the client is a self-assessment that is congruent with his observation. Clients must be convinced of their worth in a way that agrees with their own standards, if it is to be long-lasting.

Coping questions, when used properly, can be empowering and uplifting for the client. The goal for the worker, as with all the other techniques described in this book, is to help the client discover his own resources and strengths he did not know that he had. Study the following scenario and weigh the options available to you.

> Client: It's no use. I have messed up my life and nothing is going to get better. Maybe I am just "no good and will never amount to anything" like my mother always told me.

At this point, the worker has several options:

> a. to try to reassure him one more time and see what happens;
> b. to change the subject and distract him to some other topic;
> c. to reframe the strong faith he has in his mother's assessment of him as an expression of his loyalty toward his mother;
> d. to use coping questions (as follows).

Case Example

> Worker: Since you are the kind of person who believes what your mother said about you, I can see how discouraged you can become about yourself. So, tell me, how do you keep going, day after day, when there seems to be no hope? How do you even manage to get up in the morning?
>
> Client: I don't get up everyday like I should.
>
> Worker: How did you manage to get yourself up this morning?
>
> Client: I forced myself to get up because the baby was hungry and she was crying.
>
> Worker: I can imagine how tempted you must have been to

just give up. What did you do to get up and feed your baby?

Client: Well, I had to. I love my baby. I don't want her to be hungry.

Worker: Is that what keeps you going, that you love your baby?

Client: That's the only thing that keeps me going. I don't want her to live with my mother if I'm not here.

Worker: You must love your baby very much. You are a very loving mother, aren't you?

Client: Well, that's the only thing that keeps me going.

From this exchange, you can see that the worker accepted the client's view that she believed in her mother's saying that she was "no good and will never amount to anything," and went beyond it by forcing her to come up with her own reason for getting up everyday—her love for her baby. Until then, the client had not thought about this aspect of herself, that she loves her baby enough to get up everyday.

The next task for the worker is to expand on this, to build on it.

Worker: So, what would it take you to keep doing what you've been doing?

Client: I will just have to force myself to do it. I will just have to remember that my baby needs me.

Worker: So, what would it take you to convince yourself that you are a good mother to your baby?

Client: I do all I can right now. I don't listen to my mother no more. I used to believe that, but I decided that she doesn't really know me. I don't want my baby to turn out to be like me.

The client is beginning to map out what is good for her baby and making some decisions for her baby's sake. Meanwhile, the worker is helping her to assert herself by feeling comfortable about having different ideas from her mother's. There are many small things she is doing that are good for her, such as her decision not to "listen to my mother no more." The worker can start to build on her strengths, that is, her desire to do well with her baby, using this as a motivating force. Once she begins to feel good about herself as a mother, she will begin to make decisions based on her self-image as a "good mother." Another example of using coping questions to turn a hopeless and overwhelming situation into something workable follows:

Client: I was beat up by my father when I was growing up. When he got drunk, he would wake me up in the middle of the night, holler at me, beat me up for no reason. He called me names. My mother would be so scared that she didn't say anything. She'd tell me to just do what my father wanted me to do, that I should let him molest me when he got drunk. Now, I don't trust men. I don't know how to love them, I don't know how to find a good man. I am like my mother. I let men use me, and they take advantage of me. George will beat the crap out of me if I don't give him money so he can get his drugs. But I make sure that he don't get near my daughter.

Worker: How did you learn to cope with such a terrible situation all by yourself, with no help?

Client: I had to. I had no choice, did I?

Worker: I'm amazed that you not only cope with such a terrible situation with George but you have enough sense to protect your daughter so that she doesn't get abused like you did. How do you do it?

This establishes the idea that the client has considerable strengths and resources to build on. The worker can then expand on the client's strength.

Worker: So, how did you figure out that you wanted to be a different kind of mother to your baby than your mother was to you? Where did you learn to do that?

Client: Well, I watched other people, read magazines, watched TV programs, and I think about it all the time.

Worker: You are a very thoughtful person. Have you always been that way, or is it something you learn to do?

Client: I had to learn myself. Nobody taught me how to do it.

Worker: That's fantastic. I'm sure someday, your baby will learn that from you.

As you can see from this exchange, even though the client feels hopeless about herself, the worker began "where the client was" and went on to help her discover her fierce love for her child and her drive to become a different kind of mother than her mother was to her. This is a powerful discovery for the client. (More on when and how to use "coping questions" will be shown when we discuss crisis management.)

"How Do You Do It?"

You may have already noticed in this chapter the frequent question, "How do you do it?" or "How did you do it?" This question, when asked with appropriate intonation and facial expression has been found to be the most "empowering" question anyone can ask a client who has been repeatedly given a message that he is inadequate. In order to answer this question of "how," the client is forced to think about the resources and ingenuity with which he has confronted a difficult situation. I have found that clients become reassured when the worker is not making more demands, but instead highlights his strength and successes. It generates "solution talk" (Furman & Ahola, 1992) instead of problem talk. The more the client engages in the solution talk, the more clues he will generate on what to do.

When, Not If

You may also have noticed, in the examples in this chapter, many instances of the worker asking questions that start with *"When* things are better . . . ," "*When* you move up from 5 to 6 . . . ," "*When* you pretend the miracle has happened . . . ," "Who will be the first to notice *when* you feel better about yourself?"

The use of *when*, and not *if* offers the subtle but powerful implication that the changes described are bound to happen in time. The feeling conveyed to the client is that "of course it will happen" or "of course you will make these changes, it's only a matter of time." Use *when* whenever possible to convey to the client that he will make the necessary changes.

Conversely, since *if* conveys doubt and pessimism, it is useful when the worker wants to express doubts about a client having a setback, a slip, or a minor relapse. This will be particularly useful when the client's history indicates that he has made many successful attempts but has been unable to maintain them. When the client is aware of his own weakness or vulnerability, he may be able to prepare himself, to prevent falling into the same trap again. *If* is also used to caution a client about normal setbacks and the ups and downs of everyday life. When he is reminded of the normal good days and bad days of everybody's everyday life, he is less likely to panic or overreact to them when they occur.

Frequently, a client who has recently started to abstain from drug or alcohol use has unrealistically high confidence that he can maintain his "clean" life by simply maintaining a high level of "strong will." In such a situation, you might want to say things like, "*If* you are to have a setback, do you have any idea what will the first small sign to you?" Or "If you have a setback and your depression starts to come back, what do you need to do to catch yourself so that you don't go all the way down?" "*If* I were to ask your mother, what do you suppose she will say is the first thing she will notice that will tell her that you are beginning to do poorly?"

When you think the client is not clear about what the early signs of a minor setback might be, it will be valuable to discuss two things:

a. concrete clues and early signs
b. how he will manage it *if* it comes

(For more ideas on how to manage the setback when it actually occurs, see Chapter 10 on drug and alcohol abuse.)

HOW TO END AN INTERVIEW

The closure of a session is just as important as the beginning. It is important to end the session not only with an upbeat note and a feeling of having accomplished something, but with some concrete plans for what is going to happen between sessions: that is, what step is required next to move toward the goal.

As you plan to wind down the session, the following ideas will help increase your effectiveness:

1. Assess the length of the session: How long is appropriate?
2. Review the goal for the session: Have you achieved what you and the client set out to do?
3. Review the next step: Where do we go from here? What is client's task? What is your next task?
4. How close are we to termination?

The Length of an Interview

Unlike the common belief that the more "needy" the client, the longer time you must "give" to him, I contend that more is not necessarily better. Sometimes a 30-minute session of focused effort is much more effective for the client than an hour or two of meandering around various issues with no focus. Especially for those clients who have difficulty concentrating, it is much better to have a brief review of what the task was, what the result was, and what the next step will be, and end the session. This is more productive, professional, and a more economical use of the worker's time.

Summarize the Session

At the end of the interview, it may be useful to review what was discussed during the session and remind the client of the task and what the next step is. Then decide on the next task and set up the next appointment.

During the summary, be sure to cover the following:

1. Remind the client of his successes, tasks accomplished, how hard he worked, how much he cares about his children, all the good things he has accomplished and his strengths. Again, all clients need reminders about these because it is difficult for them to see their own achievements.

2. The client needs to be praised for any tasks he did, either on his own or as a result of following your suggestions. Always attribute a positive motivation for his willingness to do the task. If he followed your suggestion with some modifications, praise his common sense, intelligence, and intuition, to have done things in his own way. Give him the credit even if the credit is yours. (For those situations where the client does not do the task, see Chapter 8 for what to do.)

Case Example

> Worker: Suppose when we started, your problem with Tommy was at 1 and where you wanted to be was at 10, how far do you feel you have come between 10 and 1 today?
>
> Client: I would say it's at 6. He still don't clean his room.
>
> Worker: Of course, he is a teenager. How have you and Tommy done so much? That's very high, considering he is a teenager. What will he be doing different when you can say you are at 7?

You can give some informal education about unrealistic expectations client have of themselves or of their children by agreeing with them and then "normalizing" what they are complaining about (see Chapter 9 on "normalizing").

Compliment at the End of a Session

The compliment could be something as simple as, "You have come a long way, and you are doing many good things for your children, like making sure that they get to school on time. It takes a lot of commitment and caring on your part and I'm just really impressed by you. Keep doing it. You are doing well. I know someday your children will realize how much you've done for them." This is probably rare appreciation, the kind of "pat on the back" they don't usually get from anyone, especially from the "social worker from the welfare department."

Reminder about Termination

As each session becomes an occasion for evaluation and review of progress, both the worker and client are reminded about how close they are coming to termination. Use of the scaling question will give the worker a good measure of how the client assesses his readiness for ending the contact. The worker can also imagine a score of his confidence on safety issues, and other goal achievements. Any termination should not come abruptly at the end of a set period and it should not come as a surprise, either. Termination does not mean that the client will never have problems again, it just means that the client has solved small but significant problems, and, in the process, he learned a great deal about how to find solutions.

7

Conducting a
Family Session

In this chapter, the term "family" is used to mean both the cross-generational unit, whether through legal, biological, or sociological choice, as well as the same generation unit, and whomever the client designates as her "family." In some cultures, the "family" may mean the affectional unit, which includes close friendships. We will use the client's definition of the "family."

Gathering together the members of a large family, as well as other interested persons in the client's life is not an easy task to accomplish. It requires much coordination of everyone's schedules, arrangements for transportation, child care, and the good will of everyone involved. Most families are already under a great deal of stress and the demand of gathering every member can be quite burdensome. The family session can take place when:

a. the client decides to bring her family members, either because the family member is problematic or because she believes that family member will be helpful in solving problems.

b. you request the client to gather together certain designated family members to be present for the session, implying to the client that either the family member is a help or a hindrance to achieving the client's goals.

Some FBS, inpatient, outpatient, or residential treatment programs make the family involvement a necessary condition for participation in the treatment program. Again, I caution against making a blanket policy of requiring every family member to be present at every family session. Realistically, even if you make it a requirement, it does not guarantee compliance. Contrary to the conventional notion that family treatment can only be carried out when every family member is present, I contend that the relationship questions (discussed in detail in Chapter 6) bring the absent members into the interviewing room.

Whatever the situation, the family session can be very productive when conducted well. It depends a great deal on your skill in capitalizing on whatever goodwill there is among the family members and toward you. This chapter will describe ways to conduct the session in such a manner that it produces a positive outcome.

LENGTH OF TIME

To maximize the benefit of the session, allow yourself and the family about 1 to 1½ hours for a session. Less than this is usually not enough; a longer period makes it difficult to hold everyone's attention. In addition, longer is not always better. In an acute crisis situation, however, you may need longer to arrive at some resolution of the crisis.

HOW TO BEGIN

If you called the meeting, there should be some introductory comment from you about why you called the meeting and what you hope to accomplish by it. You can also ask them if they have any concerns about the family member with "the problem." Since you want to "join" with each member present, you need to thank them for coming, and offer some comment about how much they must care about the client, as they were willing to extend their help by attending the session. It is also a good idea to elicit each participant's idea about what they hope to accomplish through such meetings. If the family requested the session, you certainly need to comment on their goodwill and their interest in the welfare of the client.

NEUTRAL POSITION OF THE WORKER

It is important to maintain a neutral position during the family session by seeing the value in each participant's point of view. Once you take sides with someone, you are likely to lose your effectiveness. This can happen without your being aware of your own behavior. You might get a nagging feeling that something is not quite right. Do not ignore these important intuitive cues.

So, how can you tell you are taking sides? The first clue is that you begin to think like one of the family members: You start to blame someone in the family, think in "right and wrong" terms, or become emotionally upset with some member of the family. Another important clue is that you start to find faults with one member of the family. You say to yourself or to others how "disturbed" one family member is, how "serious" the problem is, or you spend too much time analyzing one member of the family.

What should you do when you become aware that this is happening to you? First, consult with the team, supervisor, or consultant between sessions. Second, review your notes and look for something good that the "problem" person is doing, however small. Thinking about how you would reframe what that person is doing as positive is also a good technique. If you feel strongly identified with one side of the family against the other, you need to remember about how a larger picture of the system might fit together. Keep trying until you get it right and feel comfortable with it. For example, if you find yourself being critical of a parent for the "inappropriate" or "unreasonable" way she deals with a child, you may want to think about how difficult the child may be to this particular parent.

MAKE CONTACT WITH EACH PERSON

Make sure you take time to establish personal contact with each person by asking what his or her interest is, what he or she does that is fun, is good at, and so on; this conveys to them that you are interested in each as a person. Again, remember to use everyday conversational language in a casual, relaxed manner. This conveys your authority and expertise in a personable, friendly way.

WAYS TO CONTROL THE FLOW OF CONVERSATION

Sometimes, conducting a family session is like being a traffic cop. Interaction among family members seems to have a life of its own. And, indeed it does. With or without you there, family life goes on; it had been there before you arrived and it will continue long after you leave. Your goal is to minimize family conflict, enhance their chances of staying connected, increase positive feelings, improve their ability to solve problems on their own, and improve their functioning.

The decision to include small children in family sessions depends on your focus and the goal of the session and how helpful or distracting the presence of children is for what you are trying to accomplish. If the child is the focus of the work, you certainly may want to include her if she is old enough to express herself. Sometimes it works better when small children are excused from the session.

The level of noise or disruptive interaction between family members certainly must be minimized in order for the session to be useful. There are no hard and fast rules about it; you must use your own judgment about what needs to be done. It is always better for the parents to control their own children, perhaps with worker's help, than for the worker to try to control the child directly. The task of the FBS is to *empower* parents so that they feel competent about themselves and so that they can be in charge of their lives, including children.

THE FOCUS OF THE FAMILY SESSION

In the family session, you need to have a clear sense about where the strength is, who is most willing to help, what is the family's view of the "miracle" picture, and what the first step is for those present.

In the session, it is important for the worker to respect the family hierarchy. Because in family relationships the parents have more power than their children — and if they don't they certainly should — more influence, and hopefully the capacity and willingness to help their children do better, it is important to make sure that they experience the worker as wanting to support them in parenting more successfully and as understanding the difficulties of their job.

This can be accomplished through addressing the parents first or taking a position of consulting the parents about what is good for their children and giving credit to them for having done some good things with their children. When referring to the parent in front of the children, it is more respectful to call them "Mother," "Father," "Mom," or "Dad," instead of calling them by their first names because this clearly indicates to them that your role is to support the parents, not to replace them.

Ways to Control Intense Emotions

All families have had a long and varied history before you came on the scene, and this history will continue long after their contact with you ends. All families have both positive and negative feelings toward each other, and through sharing sadness, tragedy, or triumph can stimulate care, concern, and acceptance of one another. Some issues can create a volatile, intensely emotional reaction of frustration, anger, or disappointment.

Emotional outbursts in the session are rarely helpful unless you have some definite strategy and the skills to control and use the outbursts therapeutically for everyone's benefit. The worker must always try to find ways to "save face" for each family member, even small children. In most situations, having flare-ups without having a clear goal is not a good idea, since venting feelings for the sake of ventilation without a clear sense of how it will lead to solutions can be damaging. It may give the client the wrong impression — that venting will solve problems.

It is your responsibility to make sure that you do not open old wounds or intense emotional issues unless you have the time and skills to diffuse the situation and turn it into a positive one. Remember, the majority of violence in the family is related directly to the intense emotions that family members evoke in each other. The family session is designed to elicit *cooperative* feelings, not incite negative feelings. Eliciting negative feelings should be the means to an end, and should not be the goal.

Case Example

Sixteen-year-old Michelle had been at the New Beginning, a group home facility for delinquent adolescents for the past three months. The list of problems were long and varied: failure in school, truancy, running away, drug dealing and alcohol abuse, an abortion at age 15, and probation for various delinquent behaviors. After three years of trying to cope with her problems through individual and family counseling, group therapy, inpatient psychiatric hospitalization, and a transfer to three different schools, the mother filed for a CHIPS (Child In Need of Protective Service) petition and refused to take her home. The mother was convinced that she and her second husband were unable to take care of Michelle any longer and that she had to "save" the rest of the family from destruction.

The case was referred to FBS for an evaluation for a possible return home and ongoing treatment, if needed, since Michelle now said she wanted to go home. Her mother was beginning to think that it might work out, based on several successful weekend visits and Michelle's expressed desire to come home. Another important factor in considering a return home was the mother's fairly stable recovery from her past alcohol abuse.

The family session was held at the group-home facility; Michelle, her mother, and her stepfather were present. The other two children were in school, and Michelle's biological father was said to have had no contact with the children for years.

The following dialogue shows how the family session can be conducted in such a way as to focus on pre-session change, exceptions to problems, and building on those small but successful accomplishments of the family members.

Worker: (*to Mother*) So what have you noticed different about Michelle that gives you the idea that it might work out this time when Michelle returns home?

Mother: She seems to have calmed down more. She is not so crazy about going out on weekends when she comes home, she is nicer to other people in the family. Her friends don't call at all hours of the night. I guess she generally stays put and acts like she wants to be part of the family.

Worker: (*to Michelle*) Is that right? How are you doing that?

Michelle: It's not that hard. I want to go home now. It's really boring here. I stay in my room a lot. I don't belong here, I should be home.

Worker: I'm curious about what made you decide that you want to go home now?

Michelle: I'm tired of running, tired of getting in trouble, and I decided I want my life to be different.

Worker: (*to Mother*) Is this new for Michelle to say this to you?

Mother: It's really different for her to say that, but I still don't trust that it's going to stay that way.

Worker: Of course, I don't blame you. So, what do you need to see Michelle do different that will tell you that things are really different this time and it will work out?

Mother: I know that she is a teenager and don't expect her to be perfect but she has to stop using the drugs and stay in school.

Michelle: But I haven't used drugs for two months and I'm getting A's and B's in school here.

Worker: You did what? You did all of that by yourself? Gosh, that's quite an accomplishment. Not using drugs for two months is a long time, especially when you are bored being here. How do you do it?

Michelle: I just don't. I just stay away from the kids who use drugs and stay in my room.

Worker: I know it's not hard to get drugs here. When you are stuck in here, it's harder to say "no" to drugs. So, how do you do it?

Michelle: Once I make up my mind, it's not hard to do. Last year I didn't use drugs for six months.

Worker: How did you do that?

Mother: That's when she was pregnant.

Michelle: When I knew I was pregnant, I didn't want to use drugs any more, so I just stopped it.

Worker: That's incredible. You must be a strong person.

Stepfather: She sure can be when she wants to be.

Worker: So, what is Michelle like when she is strong?

Stepfather: She can be a lot of fun. She makes everybody laugh. She is a good-hearted kid inside.

Worker: So, what do you notice about Michelle when she is good-hearted, and when she shows a sense of humor?

Stepfather: She helps everybody. She is very sensitive and gets upset easier than other kids. She has a way of saying things that are really grown up sometimes.

After continuing with the description of changes Michelle had made, the next step was to describe how other people were participating in the changes—the "ripple effect." The mother's criteria for Michelle's coming home were still that she must stay drug free and stay in school. Both were good goals, that is, fairly easy to measure, monitor, and they clearly would be good for Michelle. The worker needed to talk about the "ripple effect" in such a way to convey that changes are not dependent on Michelle only but on other members of the family as well.

> Worker: Tell me, Michelle, what do you notice different around the house when you are helpful, easy to get along with and fun to be around?

> Michelle: Well, Mother doesn't yell at me anymore, Mom and Tom are getting along better, and it's nice to be home. I don't feel like I have to run away or something.

> Worker: Would you say these are the things you noticed since Mom stopped drinking or were some of these there before?

> Mother: I have to admit I was in pretty bad shape. We (*pointing her finger at Tom and herself*) fought a lot, and it didn't help the kids. I just couldn't cope with all the problems. It was bad enough that we fought, but Michelle's problem didn't help at all. Sometimes, I'd fight with both of them.

At this point, it would have been easy for the worker to focus on problems since the family members seem to want to open up the issues. Focusing on a problem usually implies that there is a direct cause; someone is responsible for the problem and someone is at fault. Whenever families concentrate on problems, the conversation in the family session rapidly deteriorates into arguments, defensiveness, and blaming.

> Worker: So, what will have to be different for all three of you to say that "maybe things will work out this time," that is, for Michelle to stay away from drugs and to stay in school and for you to have things under reasonable control?

> Michelle: Well, I am talking to my P.O. about going to the alternative school and I know some kids at the NA that I used to belong before.

Mother: I know I have to keep going to AA. Maybe Tom and I
   need some help in how not to get into it in front of the
   kids.

As you can see from this interchange, clear ideas about what
has to be different and who has to do what in order to maintain
the change, were emerging from the family. Michelle was already
making some plans for school and for how she would stay drug
free. Mother was also realizing that she had to do her part to
continue to abstain from her alcohol abuse by attending AA and
that there were some issues in her marriage that needed further
work. The next task for all the family members was to find ways
to stay on the right track, to increase the successes, and to get
back on the track if they falter. The worker's job was to monitor
their progress, encourage them, and offer various ways to stay on
track.

Case Example

Helen, a 31-year-old mother of three children, ages 12, 10, and 5,
came to the attention of the Child Protective Services (a third
time for this case) because of her frequent disappearances, often
for two or three days at a time, during which she would go on
drinking binges. The most recent episode had been reported by
Helen's mother.

Helen had a continuing on-and-off relationship with Pete, who
had been in trouble with the law for possession of drugs and
dealing, a number of DWI (Driving While Intoxicated) violations, theft, and other legal and alcohol-related problems. The
financial assistance department of the public welfare tried to establish the paternity of her three children in order to force the
father to pay child support. Even though Pete was the father of
all children, Helen consistently claimed that she was too drunk to
know who the father was in order to protect him from having to
pay the child support.

Helen met Pete at age 16 and fell madly in love with him.
Pete had psychologically abused Helen, and often threatened to

abandon her. From time to time Pete would refuse to give her any money for the children and had several girlfriends "on the side."

The worker asked questions to assess Helen's perception of their relationship.

> Worker: What do you suppose Pete would say, if he was here and I were to ask him, whether you love him more or he loves you more?
>
> Helen: He would definitely say that I love him more than he loves me.
>
> Worker: Who would he say needs the other person more, you need him more, or he needs you more?
>
> Helen: I know he will say that I need him more than he does me.
>
> Worker: On the scale of 1 to 10, 10 means high and 1 means low, where do you suppose Pete will say he is at for being willing to change?
>
> Helen: I, uh, would say he is at 2.
>
> Worker: How much confidence do you have that he will change?
>
> Helen: I would say maybe 1 or 2 at most.

These scaling questions helped Helen recognize that she must change first instead of waiting for Pete to become "good," which may never happen.

The case was transferred to FBS about one week after the CPS worker's investigation, which had indicated that Helen's binge episodes had become more frequent. The FBS team decided to take advantage of Helen's remorse and offered service to her immediately. Realizing how close to losing her children she was, Helen decided to accept the service and to do something about her problem.

Because Helen's relationship with her mother was very close

(both agreed that they talked to each other 5–10 times each day), the team decided to evaluate the mother-daughter relationship to assess whether mother was "enabling" Helen's alcohol abuse and also to find out in what ways her family could be a resource for Helen's recovery.

The family session with Helen, her mother, Jackie, and sister, Kelly (eight years younger), and their small children was held at Jackie's house. The session revealed that Jackie hated Pete "with a passion," that, over the years, everyone in the family, had repeatedly advised Helen to leave Pete, because he was "using her," he "jerks her around," he will never commit to the relationship and Helen will be better off leaving him. The session included a touching expression of much caring and closeness and a demonstration of their sense of humor. They were able to laugh and talk about shared good times. All of them shared a cry about the painful reality that Helen and Kelly's brother is dying of cancer, and it was reaffirmed that Jackie was "right there" whenever Helen needed her.

Helen recognized that Pete was not good for her, but she needed to get her "act together" before anything else, which meant that she needed to control her binge drinking. She was clear that she did not want to "lose the family ties" with her mother and sister, which she had come to recognize as being very strong.

As this case demonstrates, it is difficult to expect most families to participate in family sessions every time. However, when handled well, family sessions can have a powerful impact on the client and the family unit as a whole.

Conducting a Family Session without the Entire Family

I am frequently asked about my willingness to conduct a family session without all the family members present. You may ask, "How can you do it?" or "Is it family therapy you are doing?" Before you decide to impose an undue burden on yourself and the family, a review of the dialogues throughout this book will indicate that the worker asks the client's perceptions about her significant other's perceptions of the relationship.

Since relationships are made up of predictable, repetitive, ac-
tion-reaction patterns that occur over time, even when you have
only one partner who is willing to work on solving the family
problems, there is much you can do. Just make sure that you use
the assessment outline in this book and go over it again, target-
ing the solution finding. When one person in the family makes
changes, the other has to react to them, thus disrupting the dysfunctional and nonproductive patterns of interaction.

Whether accurate or not, your client's perceptions become her
reality, that is, what she sees is what is. The way the client sees
how others in her environment see her becomes reality for her.
The relationship questions described throughout this book encourage the client to become detached enough to observe herself as
others do, while it helps the client to articulate how she assesses
her significant others. It is easy to understand then how the absent
family member's views, feelings, and behaviors are brought into
the session. Since the client's life is continuously intertwined with
those of her family members it is important that you include this
aspect in the discussion. The answers to these relationship questions are usually accurate and form the basis for the client's reality; solutions can emerge from these perspectives.

For example, in the case example above, even though Pete was
absent from the session, asking Helen about what Pete might say
about certain topics is the worker's way of bringing Pete into the
session. Listen to the following conversation and you can easily
imagine the perception of the absent spouse.

Worker: What do you suppose your husband would say needs
to change for the two of you so that you can talk to each
other more?

Client: He would say I need to slow down and not jump to
conclusions. He says I don't ask him about what he thinks
but he says I put words in his mouth. He will say I need
to listen better.

Worker: Is he right about that?

Client: Yeah, I do tend to jump on him. I need to slow down

and let him finish his sentence. But you know, he don't say anything unless I try to drag it out of him.

The client steers away to "problem talk" by describing their established pattern of interactions, in which she pursues him and the husband withdraws. It would be very tempting for the worker to be sidetracked by this problem pattern but the worker stays on course for the exceptions to her tendency to "jump" on her husband.

Worker: So, what do you suppose he would say what you are like when you slow down a bit and listen to him more?

Client: I'm not sure what I'm like when I slow down. It takes him so long to come out with his ideas and before I know, I start to tell what I think he thinks. Then he just clams up.

Worker: What do you suppose your children would say what you are like when you slow down a bit?

Client: They would say I nag too much. I'm not sure if they think I slow down ever. I am more worried about my 16-year-old son. He is just like his father. He don't say much either.

You can almost hear the one-sided conversation between this client and her family. In this process of answering questions, the client is forced to think about the absent members' portion of the dialogue.

CONDUCTING COUPLE SESSIONS

Because of the nature of the AFDC (Aid to Families with Dependent Children) system, some women clients are likely to be somewhat secretive about their liaison with men out of fear of losing their benefits. Therefore, if you encounter a partner during a home visit who you did not know was living there, be prepared to conduct a couple session spontaneously.

So, how difficult and complex is it to conduct a couple session? It certainly requires more concentration and focus than working with a single person because you are working into a relationship. Treating the couple relationship is very different from treating two individuals at the same time: It requires you to keep track of the interaction patterns and the flow of spoken and unspoken rules of the relationship while assessing the strength, affection, and commitment of both partners. The focus is always on the reciprocity, the give and take of the relationship; it is a joint enterprise with the common goal of benefitting both of them as well as the children.

When conducted properly, the couple session can result in long-term benefits for the welfare of the children. When the client feels competent about the important relationships in her life, she is more likely to parent well. When you utilize the existing resources, your work is more likely to be easier and the payoff greater.

When Is a Couple Session Useful?

As you would with the family sessions, you may request a couple session whether they are co-habitating or not. The following are guidelines that tell you that a couple session may be helpful.

1. When it is clear that the client's relationship with her partner is creating many problems for her and is affecting her ability to parent.
2. When the parent-child problem seems to be aggravated by the presence of a third person — i.e., mother's boyfriend or a stepfather.
3. When the client appears overly protective or secretive about her relationship with her partner.
4. When the client's relationship with her partner appears abusive, or involves drug or alcohol abuse.
5. When the client's child is drawn into the couple's conflict in an effort to protect the mother.
6. When the client's extended family's rejection of the partner alienates her from her family and any support they might provide.

Ways to Include the Spouse in Session

Many people regard the social worker from the Welfare Department as a "busy body" or "baby snatcher" and try to avoid running into "case workers" of any kind. Unless they have been "in the system" for various reasons, most men would rather avoid "social workers," including FBS workers, since they don't quite understand how one is different from the other. Therefore, including men in the session may be somewhat difficult initially and may require a gentle approach and persistence. The following are some helpful techniques:

1. Ask the client who helps her out the most. Talk about her needing help with raising children as a natural thing, that all mothers need to get away from their children from time to time, and that her need for an adult relationship is natural.

2. Take a stance that "it is natural to have a relationship with a partner," ask about her social life, how she manages being lonely, who helps her out financially and with the children.

3. If she indicates that there is trouble with her partner, ask about his perception of the situation, using relationship questions, such as, "If he were here, and if I were to ask him what it would take for the two of you to get along better, what do you suppose he would say?"

4. Ask her perception of his view of other things as well. This strongly suggests to the client that you value his opinion, even though he is absent and suggests to her that his view will play an important part in finding solutions.

5. When you let her know that you value her partner's opinion, unlike her family who has no use for him, she is more likely to allow him to participate in treatment.

6. If you unexpectedly run into the partner during a home visit, invite his input with respect and appreciation. Focusing on finding solutions to their difficulties bypasses the issue of blame, thus enabling them to move on to more constructive tasks.

7. If he participates reluctantly, stay with the safe topics first, such as the management of the children. If the couple indicates

that they are not ready to reveal their conflict, respect your intuitive judgment and do not be intrusive. Premature probing and any hint of you taking sides with the woman may cause the partner to not return to the next session.

Neutrality

As mentioned in the previous section on conducting family sessions, maintaining neutrality is crucial to a successful outcome in all cases. However, in couple sessions, neutrality (that is, not taking sides with either party in a dyad) is more difficult, since many couple relationships reflect some aspect of the worker's own personal relationships.

When you find yourself taking sides, or even leaning toward thinking that one or the other side in a dyad is "more right" or "more at fault," always try to keep in mind the "flip side" of one's point of view. Nothing that happens in personal relationships occurs in a vacuum. Whatever the problem, both sides are "victims" of their perceptions and, therefore, they try doing "more of the same" things that do not work. Again, avoid doing what everyone else has tried and failed. For example, if the father takes a stand that the child should be handled with a "firm" hand while the mother insists that a "soft" approach will work out better with a particular child, the worker will be more productive when he can see the value as well as the problems of both approaches. Unless there is a safety issue involved, the neutral position you take will increase your ability to influence both parents. Both approaches have merit and problems when carried to an extreme, therefore, your task is to help them come toward the middle ground, not insist that one is "right" and one is "wrong."

Conflicting Goals

One of the issues that confuses workers most frequently when working with couples is the issue of what they want from treatment. The nature of the complaint usually seems to indicate that each wants the other to change and that if only that were to happen, their relationship would be fine. FBS workers know that clients can only change themselves and that relying on and waiting for others to change makes our clients feel helpless and out of control. Therefore, a request that you change a client's spouse not only is impossible but also increases the conflict and feelings of helplessness. Be sure to assess accurately that their demand for the partner to change is not a momentary emotional outburst. Frequently, such angry demands may stem from pent up frustration. Use of scaling questions will give you a good sense of how realistic is the client's evaluation of the partner's willingness, readiness, ability, and desire to change or to make things better.

What appear to be opposite goals can usually be viewed as two different approaches to the same goal. For example, if Betty wants Lou to talk to her more instead of being "glued to the TV," while Lou wants Betty to give him a chance to approach her on his own, what seems contradictory wishes are actually two aspects of the same thing: to get along better. Therefore, the worker can help the couple realize that each has different ideas of how to achieve the same goal or more peace and harmony. Again, the scaling question discussed earlier in Chapter 6 will give you a good assessment of how willing they are to work to achieve what they both want. As long as the couple indicates that they are invested in staying together and making the relationship work, many of your reframing skills will be helpful to point out that they want the same goal.

The initial important component of assessment in a couple relationship is to figure out how much "goodwill" or positive regards and affection there is in the couple. When you get a feeling that the partners really like each other, and there is general positive regard for each other, then any disagreement between them can be reframed as two approaches to the same goal. Ask the couple to put on a scale how much each thinks the other person loves him or her; who loves whom more; how much the partner would say he or she is loved. Along with other verbal and nonverbal clues you obtain from the couple, asking these scaling questions will give you some direction on how to proceed.

Case Example

> Worker: If I were to ask your husband how badly you think he wants this marriage to work, let's say that 10 stands for he will do just about anything humanly possible to make this work, and 1 stands for he can take it or leave it, what do you think he will say where he is at between 1 and 10 today?

> Wife: That's hard to answer because he doesn't say much. If I had to guess, I would say he is about 5.

> Husband: She is wrong. If I didn't want this marriage I would have left a long time ago. She wants me to keep telling her how much I love her but how many times does a guy have to repeat the same thing before she will believe me?

> Worker: *(to the husband)* So, you really love her more than she thinks you do, is that right?

> Husband: That's right. I'm the kind of guy that would have left a long time ago if I didn't want to stay.

> Worker: So, knowing her as well as you do, what do you think it will take for her to be finally convinced that you really love her?

> Husband: I wish I knew. I go to work everyday, come home everyday, trying to keep the peace in the family and not say anything about how tough it is to keep going with no education in this day and age.

> Worker: You really must love your family very much in your own way. So this family is very important to you?

> Wife: I wish we could sit and talk like this. We used to do this when we first met. That's what I liked about him.

> Worker: So what would it take for both of you to go back to doing it again?

The worker in the above example has a couple of possible options to pursue. For example, the worker could have pursued the wife's answer to the scaling question, which was 5. If the husband was silent and did not protest about his wife's answer of 5, the worker could possibly have asked what her husband would do different when she thinks he is at 6. Or the worker could have turned to the husband and asked him about where he thought his wife was on the same scale. But in this example, the worker decided that the husband's protest about his wife's low assessment of his investment in the relationship might potentially lead to something useful. The outcome was the discovery of their earlier history of when they were able to talk more. This certainly could be productive in terms of the couple discovering what worked for them in the past.

Not all options available to the worker lead to such positive outcomes; you may need to just persist and try something else until you find a path that will eventually lead to something productive, that is, some path that will instill some hope and offer possibilities for the clients to try and discover better ways to accomplish what they want.

The following case example shows how the worker was able to look at the presenting complaint from a slightly different point of view from that of the couple and thus was able to help the couple achieve what they wanted: to live a more satisfying life with each other because they loved each other.

Case Example

Leroy (age 26) and Lucinda (age 27) had been together for about three years and had been married for about a year. Lucinda had a seven-year-old child from her previous relationship. They reported that they used to be physically abusive to each other but somehow learned to stop that. Instead, they screamed, yelled, and argued so loudly that they had been evicted once and were concerned about another eviction. After about a year of working for a temporary job service, Leroy finally got a permanent job, which he wanted to keep badly.

The presenting issue was that Leroy suspected that Lucinda might be "fooling around" when she goes out with her girlfriends. Lucinda denied this. Every time Lucinda returned from her evening out with her girlfriends, she found Leroy home, brooding, and sulking, and they end up fighting each time.

The couple said they loved each other and both wanted to make the marriage work. From various signs, it was clear that they did love each other and were greatly pained by the fights. Even though he was quiet spoken, Leroy was no pushover and stood his ground; Lucinda, on the other hand, was outspoken with her opinions, but she was not about to back down from her position either. When asked who would be willing to go first to make things better, after a thoughtful pause by both, Leroy volunteered that he would take the first step to make things better between them. Lucinda promised that she would take the second step if Leroy took the first. The worker decided to positively use the couple's competitive style of relating to each other. The worker gave the following feedback and suggestion to the couple.

"It is very clear to us (the FBS team) that Lucinda is a very strong-willed person, and it takes a strong man to love a strong women. We can see you two are a good match and can make this marriage work, even though it will take lots of hard work. It is clear to us that Leroy is terribly important to Lucinda, since what Leroy does or does not do, says or does not say, has such an impact on her. And the same goes for Leroy. What Lucinda does or does not say, has such an impact on Leroy (they nod in agreement). You both are very sensitive about each other and both of you want to be loved and cared about by the other person equally.

"By the way, we like the way Leroy took the leadership position by volunteering to go first to improve things, but it is clear to us that both of you can go first. We suggest that whoever decides to take the first step does the following: Any time you sense the other person is upset, down, unsure about trusting, we want you to give the other person a squeeze of the hand, a hug, or a pat on the back without words. The other person's job is to take the second step by responding in a similar way. When we return next time, tell us what difference this makes."

The FBS team used several techniques with Leroy and Lucinda. The first was reframing. It was clear to the team that Lucinda was a strong, articulate, vocal woman who could easily intimidate most men. Leroy, on the other hand, though quiet and soft spoken, did not easily back down. The team decided to re-frame these qualities as strengths rather than as problems. Their tendencies to fight about everything, to correct, and to counter everything with their own reasoning was reframed as a sign of caring and valuing the other person's opinion.

The second technique the workers used was to call on existing strengths. Even though Leroy volunteered to "go first," the work-ers decided to use the couple's tendency to be competitive and told them either can "go first," thus using their competitiveness to increase their desire to do something to improve the relationship.

The third task the workers employed was the "do something different" task. Since their tendency to argue verbally gets the couple into trouble, the team decided to go for nonverbal ways to communicate their positive feelings for each other. Sometimes, nonverbal communication, such as a squeeze of a hand, a loving look, a gentle pat on the back can be a more profound and mean-ingful way of expressing affection.

The last task the workers used was the observation and doing task. They were asked to tell the team what difference their "do-ing something different" made. Thus, the couple was directed to look for something "different." When they look for it, they are more likely to find it (their nonverbal sign of valuing each other).

8

Middle Phase and Termination

ANY WORKER WHO HAS carried cases of some length knows that the transition from the initial phase to the middle and termination phases becomes somewhat murky. At times, it feels like you are stuck in one phase without realizing that you and your client have begun to move. Because each case is unique, such an assessment is also unique and depends on what transpires between you and your client. With some cases, the middle phase may begin as soon as the second week. Clinically, it begins as soon as an initial burst of changes toward the goals occurs, however small the step may be. This chapter will focus on types and methods of concrete suggestions you can offer to help clients reach their goals, on ways to monitor and support the progress the client is making, and on what to do if there is no progress.

ONGOING EVALUATION

Now that you have initiated some activities, the next step is to evaluate the assessment and revise the tasks, if necessary. Any additional information that was not available during the initial assessment phase may shed different light on the case. Since treatment is a constantly changing, fluid, evolving process, the worker needs to be alert to refining the goal and evaluating progress. New information not only aids in refining the assessment but also alerts the worker to any change in the desired direction and to changes in the client's life.

Evaluation not only is done at the time of termination but is an ongoing, constant process, and, therefore, it gives direction as to how you should modify and revise your goals and strategies as you go along. A good, ongoing evaluation means that there should not be any surprises at the time of termination.

Keep in mind the following criteria during the middle phase of treatment.

1. Each contact with clients should become an evaluative session. Pay close attention to how new information you may have confirms what you are doing or gives you a new idea about what to do or not to do.

2. Clients do not know what kind of information you are looking for or what will be helpful to you. Therefore, think of any additional information you receive as adding to the larger picture, these are not necessarily things they were trying to hide.

3. Some new information is useful and some not. In order to sort out what is useful and what is not, examine your treatment goal. Does this new information provide you with better ideas on how to achieve the goal for this family? Does it give you new ideas about who will be most interested in doing something about the problem?

4. Be flexible and willing to change your mind based on new information. It takes confidence in your ability and trust in your own intuition and common sense judgment to acknowledge your mistake and revise your initial impression about the goals and targets of intervention.

5. Keep the following questions in mind: Was the initial goal appropriate? Am I working with the right person? How close is the client to achieving the goal? What would be the next sign of success? *Who* has to do *what, when, where,* and *how* to move to the next step toward the goal? What needs to be revised? What can stay the same?

6. Recognize signs of a lack of progress. If you find yourself feeling frustrated with a case or feeling like you are working harder than the client, you may have reached an impasse. No need to panic. There are some steps to take to remedy this:

Do not blame or get angry at the client. It probably is neither your nor the client's fault. The client may be just as frustrated as you are. So, both of you are in it together. Mention to the client that things are not going well and that you may have made a mistake. When you involve the client in making things right, he will become more motivated to work with you. It is not all your work. Remember, clients are like anybody else and people are willing to help those in trouble when asked. It is empowering to the client to be allowed to discover his helpful, cooperative, and nurturing side.

Review your goals: Was the goal too big? Start with a small, simple one. Is the right person involved in finding solutions? What is the sign of success for a new goal?

Remind the client about his successes and accomplishments, however small.

OFFERING SUGGESTIONS AND TASKS

As an FBS worker you are in an excellent position to find solutions to clients' problems, not only because you are trained, but simply because you are in a position to stand back and observe the patterns of "more of the same" that clients tend to repeat. A good way to explain this to yourself is that clients are in the middle of a picture when they try to solve their problems. When someone is a part of a picture, it is difficult for that person to see the whole picture. But, as an outsider, you can see the whole picture much more easily and you know what needs to be done to make the picture "look right."

Since it is easier for you to see the whole picture, you can easily make the mistake of offering suggestions and advice too soon, thus becoming too impatient with the client. This phenomenon can be described as "being ahead of a client." Remember, as a worker, you have influence on the client to a point. Knowing how to pace the client's readiness to change is a skill that comes with training and experience.

Here are some guidelines for maximizing your influence on the client so that the possibility of the client following your suggestion is increased.

The Task Has to Make Sense to the Client

Even the best suggestion that the worker makes is useless if the client does not follow it. Frequently, a worker may blame the client and become frustrated and angry with him or label him "resistive," "unmotivated," and so on. This is not helpful; it might make the worker feel better for a few minutes but it will not help the client find a solution. So how do you get the client to "do something different," since everybody, including clients, does things in a certain way because it seems to be the most sensible at the time?

Before making your suggestion to the client, review it and see if you think your client will accept the suggestion as a sensible thing to do from his point of view. When you can say "yes" to yourself, then the likelihood of the client accepting your suggestion will increase.

What to Do

Be patient. Do not jump into offering advice or suggestions. Take some time to study the situation, ask questions that the client did not think of asking himself. Listen attentively first. Find out what he is doing that is good for him.

Challenge the way the client constructs or explains the problem. Gently start to put some doubt into the way the client conceptualizes the problem if the client's way of thinking about the problem is not helping him find solutions.

Case Example

Client: You know, the reason Tyron talks back to me is because he hates me. I can just see the hatred in his eyes and the stuff he says. I didn't teach him that way. I always tell him he has to respect his mother. I am his mother and he can't talk to me that way.

The worker has several options. Since the mother is more upset
about her son's behavior than the son is, the mother is most likely
to become a "customer" for change. As long as the mother sees the
son's behavior as "hatred" toward her, she will respond accordingly, most likely with equal intensity of anger or with punishment. Naturally, this will result in more angry exchanges, which
in the mother's mind confirms her initial view. However, if she
saw the same behavior as something other than "hatred," the
chances of her changing her interaction with her son would increase. The worker can respond to this by putting some doubt on
the mother's way of thinking.

> Worker: You think so? From what you said about Tyron so
>   far, it seems a little different from most boys hating their
>   mothers. It just doesn't sound the same to me. You know
>   I work with lots of children his age. And I met him and
>   talked to him quite a bit. He just doesn't seem like most
>   kids I work with.
>
> Client: So, what do you think it is?

If the client has come this far, that is, she has become curious
about your way of thinking about her son, the chances of her
wanting to hear your ideas about her difficulty with her son will
be increased. Most parents want to believe their children are different from other children (special) while they also want to be
reassured that they are the same (normal). At the same time, all
parents want their children to do better in life than they have
done themselves.

> Worker: It seems more like his wanting to flex his muscles a
>   little bit. It is clear that you have taught him all the right
>   values. I guess now he needs to test what he has learned.

When you make sure that the client is open and ready to hear
your ideas and when you give the credit back to the parent for
having taught the child the good things it knows increases the
chance that the client will follow your suggestions. Working with

people calls for a sensitivity to "timing." A suggestion offered at the wrong time, that is, when the client is not ready to "hear," will fall on deaf ears. This is the major complaint from parents about their preadolescent and teenage children. And workers don't need to repeat what the parents do. You will know that the clients are ready to hear you when they ask your opinion for better ideas or different ways to solve problems (see Chapter 2 on assessment of customer-type relationship).

Positively frame the motivation behind what the client is doing and give him lots of positive feedback about his past and current successes. You can always suggest that what the client is doing is his way to "improve his life," "to improve the children's lives," to "make things better," and so on. Assume that the client's motives are always for the good of his family and himself.

State the suggestion you are making as the natural next step to complete the job he started, or as the next step in making his tasks a little bit easier.

Case Example

A mother bitterly complained about her 14-year-old daughter, Cindy, who was failing in school, was continually late to school, skipped classes, and ran away when her mother tried to reprimand her. The mother's view was that she has absolutely failed to bring her daughter up properly; she felt that she had lost control of her daughter and that Cindy's "wild" behavior was caused by the "wrong friends she hangs out with." The logical response to feeling out of control is to tighten the restriction, thus creating a familiar repetitive cycle of the more mother tries to control, the harder Cindy rebels, and the less successful the mother feels.

A session with the daughter indicated that she felt helpless about her situation, got very upset that her mother called her "names," felt that "nobody cares" about her, was afraid of getting "hit on the head," and was ashamed of failing. Cindy acted "street smart" but at times seemed younger than her age; she wanted some reassurance and structure from adults.

When the mother's problem solving methods were examined closely, it became apparent that the mother needed to stop "yelling and screaming" at Cindy, to the more positive with her, to make it possible for Cindy to approach her, and to help her realize how much mother loves and cares about her welfare. The daughter needed to make some changes, also, such as staying in school, getting some help with her academic problems, being more careful about safety, and finding ways to get along with her family better.

It is important right from the beginning not to get too far ahead of the client and to introduce some doubt into the mother's view of the problem so that she can feel some control over the situation. Viewing the problem as Cindy's "bad friends" is not very useful, since the mother cannot select friends for Cindy. The mother needs to help Cindy to learn to use her own judgment and to make good decisions. How might this be done, and how might you frame positively what mother is doing?

If the client is ready, ask yourself what kind of tasks it would be appropriate to set for both mother and daughter, which will move them toward their goal.

The Worker's Task

1. Ask about any times mother and Cindy get along even for a short time. Can they do it again? If yes, suggest it as a task. If no, ask the "miracle question" to get some ideas. Be persistent in a gentle way.

2. Ask about when Cindy behaves within an acceptable range. Find out what it would take for Cindy to repeat this behavior. Find out how mother is different with Cindy at those times.

3. Was there any time when Cindy did well in school? What would it take for her to do it again?

4. Assess who is most interested in finding solutions. Work with that person closely. Find out who else can be helpful to mother.

5. Find out what is important to that person and make sure you connect with that person. Use of scaling question on motivation would be useful.

6. Find out everybody's strengths and resources. Use them.

7. Find out who tried what, how that did not work. Rule these out.

8. Establish a small, realistic, and measurable goal.

9. List the family's past successes and accomplishments.

10. Present the task as the next step in completing their ongoing effort to improve their lives.

What to Do if Client Does Not Follow Suggestions

First of all, do not panic and do not get upset with the client. When he fails to carry out the suggestions we make, there usually is a good reason for it. The following steps may be a useful guide to reviewing the situation.

1. Find out from the client what he did instead of following your suggestion. Find out all you can about what he found useful or helpful from what he did instead of following the suggestions.

2. If he did not do anything, find out if the problem is better. If it is better, find out what he did to make it better. The client may have a better solution than you have. Be open minded about it.

3. If the client did not do the task and says the problem is not better, you may have the wrong goal, or you may be working with the wrong person. Review your goal and who the "customer" is. The client may become a "customer" for his own goal.

4. If you have the wrong "customer" or wrong goal, start over and proceed with the appropriate steps.

5. Let the client know that he used good judgment by not following a suggestion he didn't feel "right" about.

6. Ask the client what *he* believes he needs to do to solve the problem.

7. Emphasize the gravity and the seriousness of the problem.

8. Maintain the attitude and posture that the client knows what is best for himself and his family.

ENHANCING POSITIVE CHANGES:
WHAT'S BETTER?

Once you can see that the client is starting to make some positive changes, the easiest and most enjoyable part of your job begins. This next step is enhancing changes and continuing to improve on the gains the client is making.

The majority of the second and subsequent contacts should begin with the question "What's been better—even a little bit better—since we got together last time?" Asking the question in this way implies that something is bound to be better and that the worker is interested in finding out what that is. This way of asking is very different from "Is anything better since we met last time?" Clearly when asked "What is better" the client is more likely to respond by saying that something is better, while "Is anything better?" implies that the worker is somewhat doubtful about improvements. Clients have varying responses: The majority will take some time to reflect on what has been better and will tell you about what has improved; others will say everything is "about the same"; the third group, which is much smaller than the other two groups, will say things are "worse." Since the majority of the clients will report things are "little bit better," let me first discuss four useful responses that should follow the client's answer: Elicit, Amplify, Reinforce, and Start again. (The team at the Brief Family Therapy Center calls these responses EARS for Elicit, Amplify, Reinforce, and Start again.)

Elicit

"What's better?" is how the worker elicits how the client made things even a little bit better on his own. Even though he may have followed the *worker's* suggestion to make things better, the credit always goes to the *client*. This process of asking and listening attentively to the answers to "How did you do that?" to someone who, for example, walked out of the house instead of "whacking" his child as he usually did, is the most respectful and empowering activity you can do for any client. In the process of explaining to you the details of his thinking, his feelings, and the behavioral processes that helped him to arrive at the decision to take a small step to make things better in his own way, he is taking ownership of the success.

When 13-year-old Liz reported that she went to school for two days and she washed the dishes once during the four days between the initial and the second session, the worker was curious about whether this was different from her usual behavior. Even though the mother was not very impressed with Liz's washing the dishes, "since it was her turn anyway," the worker was persistent in finding out how this event happened. Such questions distinguish this event as different from others, as perhaps the beginning of a new effort, or as a new and significant movement toward responsibility and maturity. With this newly heightened awareness, a common event such as washing dishes or going to school is viewed differently than before. As Liz talked about the dish washing she remembered that she got up promptly when mother called her on a school day. The worker was even more curious about how Liz managed to get up without her usual fuss and asked whether this was different for her also. Both mother and daughter had to think about this for a while and replied that indeed it was a change for Liz. Difference is what creates change, therefore, it is a concept that cannot be used too often.

Amplify

Using the dish washing and getting up on time without a battle, the worker then begins to amplify the effects of these two small events. "How did you figure out that washing dishes was the right thing to do?" "How did you manage to just go ahead and get the dishes out of the way?" "How did you know that it will help things?" "Wasn't it hard to get up on time when you did?" "Who noticed, besides Liz, that she did something different?" "What did mother do different when Liz did the dishes?" "When she got up on time?" "What impact did these events have on Liz the rest of the evening or rest of the day?" "What different did these make in the way she approached other responsibilities?" "How did this affect her interaction with her mother?" You can see how the worker can capitalize on the "ripple effect" of two minor events that the mother and the daughter may have overlooked. When Liz does the dishes or gets up without complaint again, the mother and daughter may look at each other slightly differently.

Reinforce

There are many subtle and not so subtle ways to reinforce any positive changes the client is making. Raising an eyebrow, a surprised look, confusion about what you heard, and so on, are all nonverbal ways to reinforce this as something different. "Wow" is a wonderful way to say a lot without saying a great deal. "What did you say you did?" while leaning forward with an incredulous look on your face will highlight the changes and reinforce the good decision the client made. Other reinforcing questions are: "Not everyone (your age, in your situation, with your problem, etc.) can do that. So, are you the kind of person who "just does things because it is the right thing to do"? I wonder where you learned that? Was it hard to do, I mean getting up on time? How did you force yourself to get up?"

Start Over

When the details about washing dishes or getting up in the morning are exhausted, you can start this process over by asking, "What else is better?" with an expectant look on your face. When given some time to reflect on this, the client is likely to search for something else he did to make things better. Even though she was reluctant at first to discuss the improvement, Liz's mother volunteered that Liz was good about getting off the phone when she reminded her about the time limit. The worker repeated the steps of amplifying and reinforcing until this topic was exhausted By the time these three topics were examined very carefully, in minute detail, it seemed like Liz had reached a significant turning point. Obviously, the worker needs to remind the mother that this is a very good start and that she still has a long way to go and that it will take lots of hard work.

WHEN A NEW PROBLEM COMES UP

Once the initial problem becomes less of a concern and fades into the background, clients and workers are often eager to move on to the next set of issues. It is easy to move on to the next set of problems without realizing the full impact of success once the pressure is off and there is a bit of breathing room for the client.

Make sure that you help the client to take some time out to relish and enjoy the positive changes and his successes, and of course, give credit to the client for all the positive things he has done to bring about the changes.

1. Find out in step-by-step fashion what is better with the original problem: who is doing what, when, how, and with what results. (This is useful information for subsequent problem solving, as well.)

2. Do not let the client move on to complaints about the next set of problems. Reassure the client that you will return to his concerns later, but stick to your agenda of making sure that he understands what he is doing that is different and how that is linked to success.

3. Find out what the client learned from the successes.

4. Find out what the client can remember to do next time *if* the problem comes up again.

5. Make sure that the new problem fits into the larger picture of the original goals. For example, obeying the curfew and getting off the phone are related to a teenager's learning to live with rules, or dealing with father's drinking is related to the family getting along better.

WHAT TO DO WHEN CLIENTS
REPORT NO CHANGE

Many clients and those who referred them look for immediate and massive changes. Because they may have suffered from the problem for a long time, there may be a sense of urgency about solving the problem. Giving in to such pressure to produce quick and massive changes will bring you undue stress. This is the time to slow down.

One of the most helpful tasks of the FBS is to teach clients to look for improvements. Help the client to look at each day closely, and ask her to describe the details of what each day has been like for him and his family. Instead of blurring one day into the next, this careful scrutiny of each day helps the client discover that he coped with many of life's problems. The information generated this way become the building blocks of successes. This important process teaches the client to look for and appreciate numerous small successes on the way to the bigger and better. Remember our basic assumption that change is constant and inevitable. Therefore, something small in the client's life is bound to be different, and the worker's task is to find that small change and use it as a building block to larger success.

WHAT TO DO IF CLIENTS REPORT
THAT THINGS ARE WORSE

Occasionally, some clients will answer "It's worse" when asked "What's better" during one of your middle phase sessions. In most clinical situations, the client's perception that "things are worse" is very much colored by an incident or events that occurred just prior to your meeting or some new crisis that may not be related to the goals. For example, the family had a fairly decent and peaceful five days, but for two days the tension flared again and to the client it may feel like this argument is like the other arguments they had before the FBS involvement. At other times, the client may report "things are worse" when some new issue arose immediately before your home visit and they are still in the middle of solving this problem. More frequently, however, the client's perception is colored when there was an argument during the trip to your office. Again, be persistent in finding out the details of who did what, where, when, how, and with what results, and look for ways that the family made things better, even a little bit. All your skills as "a solution detective" come into play here: Use the techniques of eliciting, amplifying, reinforcing, and starting again.

If a crisis occurs that was not part of the initial presenting problem, you may need to assess the urgency of the crisis and make appropriate decisions (see the section on "Crisis" in this chapter).

Following are postures and attitudes to keep in mind during the middle phase of treatment:

1. Do not become discouraged. Behave as if you expected the crisis, since it is really quite natural that life has ups and downs. Concentrate on how he improved things, even a little bit.

2. Ask in what specific way things are worse. Start to put some doubt into client's perceptions of how much worse things are.

3. If there is a new problem, do not hesitate to set it aside and return to the original problem the client and worker agreed to work on.

4. If it is the same problem both decided to work on, ask about the details of how, what, when, who, and in what ways things are worse.

5. Start pointing out some differences you notice and start to give client credit for having made some small changes.

6. Ask questions like, "How did you think of doing it that way?" or "Where did you come up with that idea?" or "That's great!" or "Whose idea was it that you do it that way?"

7. Using the coping question, ask how he managed to cope with such terrible situation, and accept his view without challenging him. Also ask why it is "not worse," given the terrible conditions and the enormity of the problem he faces. Whatever his answer to your coping questions, ask "What about it was helpful to you?"

8. Some clients report that nothing is better even though in reality you can see the positive changes, such as his voice is stronger, he is more active, the children are behaving better, and so on. Go back and review if you have a visitor or a complainant. You may not have a customer.

9. Meet with the client less frequently than in the beginning. When you see your colleagues or family members everyday it is difficult to see changes. It also allows the client to experience setbacks and then report to you how he managed to maintain

his composure. These are the strengths and resources he will need after you are out of his life.

AS YOU MOVE CLOSER TO THE END

Think of yourself as a coach and a consultant to your clients at this point, and the nature of your relationship with the client will change over time. Both roles have elements of teaching, nurturing, encouraging, healing, cheerleading, suggesting, and molding clients' opinions about their ability and skills. While occasionally you may insist they do things in certain ways, all good coaches know that influencing self-perception and improving self-esteem have the greatest impact on performance.

Here is a list of tasks you need to do after the initial contacts and as you begin to see some positive changes:

1. Clients often do not notice their own successes. Look for even a small change and comment on it. Examples may be as small as you noticing that the dishes are cleared away, his hair is combed, he went to church, etc., all ordinary daily routines that signal an ability to cope.

2. Look for something new to comment on and encourage during each contact you make. Clients may not be aware of these little signs of successes. With enough repetition, they may learn to do it themselves.

3. Find out what you are doing that works. However small, ordinary, or simple, keep noticing what you do that worked with a particular client or with FBS clients in general. Know your repertoire of things you do well with clients, things that work for you. Remember to use those skills when you need to.

4. A good coach gives constant feedback. Your positive feedback will help the client recognize what strength he has and what is different in his life. These are the things he can do for himself when you terminate the case. Unless the client knows what changes he is making and, therefore, what is different in his life, he will not know how to transfer his learning to other situations.

TERMINATION

There are two different ways to determine when the joint work between the worker and client is achieved: lapse of a designated time or accomplishment of the goal.

Time as an External Criterion for Termination

There are many programs that utilize number of sessions as a criteria for when to end a contact, such as insurance companies, health maintenance organizations (HMO), employee assistance programs (EAP), and some FBS programs. Clearly such an approach has positive and negative effects on the therapeutic outcome.

Mann uses 12 sessions maximum (Mann, 1973), while Sifneos limits treatment to 8 to 14 sessions (Sifneos, 1985), and Malan (1976) to 40 sessions. However, all have stringent patient selection criterion (as developed by Sifneos, 1965).

Patients must

1. be of above average intelligence,
2. have at least one meaningful relationship with another person,
3. not be in emotional crisis,
4. have the ability to express feelings and interact with the therapist,
5. be motivated to work hard during psychotherapy,
6. have a specific complaint.

It is not difficult to see the limitations of this approach. These selection criteria are difficult to enforce when working in the public sector, such as FBS, and even in some parts of the private sector, such as community mental health clinics or community agencies that are supported by public funds and, therefore, must serve everyone who comes into the clinic.

Many FBS models determine a specific number of days, such

as 30, 45, or 90 days, in order to determine how long a case will stay open. Usually, at the end of the specified number of days the case is either transferred to other ongoing programs or it is closed. This approach can be useful, since clients know exactly when the end is coming. Knowing that there is a distinct end to the contact can help to keep both the client and the worker motivated.

The problem with using time as a termination limit is that some clients will "buy time," with passive-aggressive behaviors, such as missing sessions; this can be excruciatingly difficult for both the worker and the client. Time limits can be helpful in pacing and monitoring progress. This approach also forces the client and the worker to be concise and limit the treatment goal to a manageable level.

Even when you use the number of days as a criteria for termination, it is a good idea to remind clients frequently of their accomplishments.

Goal Achievement as a Criterion for Termination

Some treatment models, such as the Mental Research Institute (MRI) model of brief therapy (Watzlawick, Weakland, & Fisch, 1974) and the solution-focused brief therapy model described earlier in this book, use specific goal accomplishment as criteria for termination. If the goal is achieved before the 10-session or 90-day deadline, for example, the case can be closed. When the goal is described in behavioral, concrete, measurable terms, it is easy to see when to terminate. In other words, the sooner the client accomplishes his goals, the sooner the contacts with the worker can end. Often this is a powerful motivator for the client.

The difficulty with using goal attainment as a criterion is that, in some circumstances, it can take some time to test the success. For example, some problems such as occasional depressive episodes, infrequent fighting between a couple, or occasional drinking binges, etc., that do not follow a repetitive, predictable pattern, it may be necessary to let some time pass after achieving success to know if enough of a solid solution pattern has been established. Obviously potentially difficult scenarios should be discussed and rehearsed with the client before termination.

Whatever the criteria you use in your own mind, it is again important to know when the contact should end. I suggest that you review the guideline for establishing treatment goals.

REVIEW OF INITIAL AND REVISED GOALS

As time goes on, you need to keep track of the initial goals agreed on by you and the client. It is useful for you to review them with the client regularly, using scaling questions. Not only do you need to ask the client these questions, but you also need to ask yourself how close you are to achieving your goals.

> Worker: I want to ask you a slightly different question. Looking back, suppose that when we first started meeting your life was at 1 and where you want your life to be at is 10. Where would you say you are at today between 1 and 10?

> Client: I would say I am at maybe 4 or 5.

> Worker: What do you suppose it will take for you to be at maybe 5 or 6?

or

> Worker: On the same scale, 10 means you have every confidence that you will continue to control your drug use, 1 means you have no confidence at all, where would you say you are today?

> Client: I would guess at 4 because I still get cravings and I still get crabby with the kids.

> Worker: So, what would it take you to move up from 4 to 5?

> Client: I have to keep going to AA and keep busy.

> Worker: Suppose your mother was here and if I were to ask her, what do you suppose she would say she needs to see you do for her to say that you are at 5?

ASSESSING THE READINESS
FOR TERMINATION

Worker: You have made a lot of changes since we started to work together. On a scale of 1 to 10, with 10 meaning you have every confidence that you will stay at 5 and 1 means you have no confidence at all, where would you put yourself between 1 and 10 today?

Client: I will say I am at 7.

Worker: I think it takes some getting used to the changes you have made. What would it take for you to stay at 7 for the next month? Two months?

Client: I will just have to keep doing what I've been doing.

Worker: If your mother were here and if I were to ask her, what do you suppose she would say you need to do to stay at 7?

Client: She would probably say that I will have to go to church, keep going to the NA, keep busy, stay away from my drug-using friends, stay in touch with her, and things like that.

Discussion of Setbacks

Worker: What would be the earliest sign to you that you are starting to slide back? What would your family notice about you that will tell them that you are beginning to slide backward?

Client: I will get moody, not see anyone, not go out, get depressed.

Worker: That sounds to me like you have already *started* to slide back. Do you know what comes even *before* that? What do you have to do so that you can catch yourself *before* you start to slide back?

You can repeat variations of these kinds of dialogues as often as you think necessary. These questions imply that the client must take the responsibility for monitoring himself, which is an empowering message. It says to the client that you trust him to look after his own best interests and that it is his responsibility to do so. These are the tools he will need to use to work with after contact with you is terminated. A minor setback or relapse is to be expected. Tell him to look at the setback as a "test before graduation," or as an opportunity to learn something new about his ability to handle tough life situations. The setback may be because of the client "having forgotten what to do," or it may be "a reminder of what he needs to remember to do."

When the client has actually suffered a setback, review the event and emphasize what he has learned from the episode. The experience can be used to plan how he is going to handle a similar situation differently.

How Close Are We to Achieving the Goals?

As you continue to evaluate the progress toward goal achievement, you need to keep an eye on the client's accomplishments. Since this is a joint activity, clients need to know what they have achieved and what more they need to do to achieve their goals.

Again, it is important to amplify client successes, however small or minor they may seem. For the client it may be the first time he has accomplished something he set out to do. Therefore, it is crucial for you and the client to jointly evaluate how far he has come and how hard he worked at it. Clients rarely hear compliments or get "a pat on the back" from the people they feel close to. Wanting to be positively regarded is a part of human nature.

WHEN AND HOW TO
INITIATE TERMINATION

Again, designating a limited number of sessions can be a good way to decide when to terminate, but a more helpful way is to review the goals and keep reminding yourself and the client of how far the client has come:

1. How does the client understand what he did to find solutions to his problem? Does he have a clear sense of what he did to help himself?
2. Is it the kind of information that can be generalized to other situations?
3. Does he have clear ideas on what may be the early signs that things may be starting to deteriorate? Does he know what to do if this were to happen?

When you are reasonably sure that you will receive positive answers to these questions from your client, then you need to go over these points with him. The process of termination is also continuous and ongoing, since you and your client will continue to measure the progress toward the achievement of goals. Using scaling questions (see Chapter 6 for details) to measure how close he feels he is coming to reaching his goal will be useful. When the client's scale is about 7 or 8 on a scale of 1 to 10 the worker can ask the client how confident he is that he can stay at this level for next week, for example.

WHAT HAPPENS WHEN YOU ARE NOT SUCCESSFUL WITH A CASE?

A valid reason for termination may be when there is no movement in a case. How will you know you are not making progress? When you become frustrated or when you feel like saying to yourself or to your colleagues, "It's like talking to a brick wall," or "It's like pulling teeth," or "I wonder what I am doing with this case," you probably are right to wonder what is going on. Do not dismiss these nagging doubts. Anyone who works with people faces these doubts from time to time. It is quite normal and does not mean that you made a mistake or that something is wrong with you. Instead of continuing to do "more of the same" of something that doesn't work, you may consider the following:

1. At the earliest indication that a case is not going well, a consultation with the team or supervisor or an outside consultant may be called for.

2. When you feel that you have exhausted all possible approaches and are at an impasse, a transfer of the case to another team or another therapist may be useful.

3. Experiment with changing the meeting location, time, or day or change whom you meet with. For example, if you always meet with the mother, ask to meet with family members you haven't seen, or even with the mother's best girl friend, a neighbor, or a pastor the client confides in. They may provide some information that may help you get "unstuck."

Reaching an impasse is not always the client's fault, nor is it the worker's. And it does not always mean that the problem is too big or that the resources are too limited, or that there is no hope. Thinking about a transfer to another therapist or a consultation sometimes opens up a whole new way of looking at the case and new ideas can emerge. Don't overlook this possibility.

4. Mismatch of worker and client can happen any time and in any program. Such occurrences are common in the field of psychotherapy and it is unethical to pretend that bad "chemistry" does not exist.

SUCCESSFUL TERMINATION

Life is full of problems to be solved and your clients are no different from anyone else. If you wait until *all* the client's problems are solved, you will never end treatment! Many "open" cases are those that workers are fearful will "blow up," and, therefore, for safety reasons, these cases are frequently kept open much longer than necessary. What is important to keep in mind is that "empowering clients" means equipping them with the tools to solve their own problems as far as possible. When they can't do it on their own, they need to know when to ask for help and where to go for help. Termination can occur when you are confident that the client will know when and where to go to seek help, and *not* when you are confident that he will never have problems. There is no such thing as a problem-free life. Remember: "Life is just one damned thing after another."

OPEN-ENDED TERMINATION

This can occur when there is sufficient change from the treatment point of view but the court's mandate is that the family maintain contact with the FBS or the social services for a much longer period. At other times, the client may need some time to build up his confidence sufficiently. In such situations, these cases may need to be referred to an on-going worker and monitored periodically. Obviously, the more flexible the FBS program funding sources, structure, and policy, the better. Frequently, the outside restrictions will play a more important role in termination than the workers or the program administrators would like to admit.

SESSION SUMMARY

Name: _____   Worker's Name: _____

Date: _____

Improvements Made to Date:	Related to Goal		Do More?		How?
	YES	NO	YES	NO	
1. _____	_____	_____	_____	_____	_____
2. _____	_____	_____	_____	_____	_____
3. _____	_____	_____	_____	_____	_____
4. _____	_____	_____	_____	_____	_____

Compliment:

Task (Suggestions):

    Client:

    Worker:

Comments:

(continued)

165

PROGRESS CHECK LIST

FAMILY NAME: _____ DATE: _____

WORKER'S NAME: _____

PREVIOUS GOALS	REGRESSION	NO PROGRESS	IMPROVING	ACHIEVED
1. _____				
2. _____				
3. _____				

NEW GOALS:

1. _____

2. _____

WHAT'S WORKNG? _____

WHAT WILL HELP? _____

_____

TERMINATION DATE AND SUMMARY:

166

9

Do Something Different

MOST FBS WORKERS WILL find the procedures outlined in this book quite useful when followed in a step-by-step fashion. The procedures are based on the three rules of solution-focused therapy:

- Rule #1. If it ain't broke, don't fix it.
- Rule #2: Once you know what works, do more of it.
- Rule #3: If it doesn't work, don't do it again; do something different.

This chapter will explain how you can do something different.

WHAT ARE THE SIGNS THAT SOMETHING DIFFERENT NEEDS TO BE DONE?

1. There are cases where it is clear to the worker that doing "more of the same" is not sufficient, and, therefor, a drastically new behavior or new pattern of interaction is called for.
2. Even though there are clearly "exceptions" to the problem the client is not ready to acknowledge them as such.
3. No matter how hard you try to uncover the exceptions, there seem to be none.

4. The imagined solution to the problems (miracle picture) seems to call for a new pattern of behavior for the client.

5. The client is clearly a "customer" and is willing to solve problems but only if the worker can come up with some creative and innovative ideas of what to do.

The following are 15 common, easy-to-carry-out interventions and suggestions that fall under the category of "doing something different." Individualizing these to fit each client's unique set of circumstances, problems, and strengths is the worker's job. Keep in mind that these do not apply to all cases or to every client. Matching the client's situation to an appropriate task to achieve the goals takes lots of practice, good judgment, skill, and creativity. Workers can take the basic principles of various interventions described here and adapt them to fit the unique situations of each family.

The selection of tasks and interventions is based on a belief that the worker should try the simplest, easiest, and most conservative approach first before trying something more elaborate.

1. Compliments

Complimenting is a process in which the worker acknowledges what the client says, feels, and believes, and affirms and respects her attitudes about various issues that brought her in contact with the FBS. It is a powerful technique that can be tried before anything else with all type of clients. Compliments alone can be a powerful intervention when you have a "visitor" or in the early phase of FBS cases. Do not underestimate their usefulness. As one abusive, violent, volatile, client in his late 40's said, "Honey works better than vinegar." (The worker complimented him on his having gained "the wisdom of life.")

So what do you want to compliment the client on? It may not necessarily be related to the problem that brought her to the attention of the FBS. Anything you notice about the client, the way she makes an effort to look nice, the way she handles her child, cleans her house, maintains a supportive social network — anything that you think will help enhance her self-esteem and competency. A colleague described this activity of looking for something to compliment the client on as "holding up a magnifying glass and picking out with a tweezers" in some situations. When the client feels better, she will eventually be able to do other positive things for herself and her children. Clients are not aware of what they routinely do; they need feedback about their successes, especially from professionals.

When you cannot think of anything else to suggest to the client, remember to compliment her especially if you get a sense that most of the client's experience with various professionals has been negative. You can compliment her on her patience in sitting through the session and answering some tough questions; what a good description she gave of her life; how the children sat through even though it must be very boring for them; how she still has hope for her difficult child in spite of negative experiences, and so on.

Clients can learn to use this approach with their children, relatives, and other important people in their lives. Workers can coach the client on using compliments with others who have influence in her life by helping her to watch for positive things that other people do. You and your clients will see the results almost immediately.

2. Intrasession Consultation

Some years ago, I met an in-home treatment team in rural France who, toward the end of the session, would ask the family's permission to use the kitchen for a brief consultation. When I train FBS workers during the home visit, we sometimes hold consultations in our car; you may want to just step outside the family home and give yourself a brief moment to think.

So, of what use is this intrasession break? It is helpful in enhancing the worker's objectivity by giving her some distance from the immediacy of the session and in increasing the impact of the session on the family.

During the face-to-face interaction with the client, especially if there is more than one member of the family present, it is not an easy task for the worker to keep track of all the activities that occur. However, with the physical distance from the family afforded by a break, it becomes somewhat easier to maintain objectivity about the interactional patterns. Taking a discussion break or reviewing a videotape of the session gives the worker a break from continuous interaction with the client and allows her some time to review the process of the session and evaluate what has taken place. Removing yourself physically from the family dynamics can relieve the pressure of having to be attentive to each and every member of the family and can help the worker "recharge," collect her thoughts, and summarize her impressions. This also decreases the likelihood of the worker getting caught up subjectively in the family's interactions.

These breaks seem also to heighten the client's expectations and curiosity about what the worker's feedback will be. People want to hear about themselves, and clients are no exception to this. Thus, the worker may notice that the clients change their postures, sit up straight, become more attentive, and concentrate on what the worker says, thus heightening the intensity of the session.

How should intrasession consultations be handled? The worker, whether working alone or with a team, can explain the procedure during the initial contact with the client. The explanation may go like this:

> I want to explain to you about what you can expect to happen. I would like to spend about 45 minutes or so talking with you about how I can be of help to you. Toward the end of the session, I will take some time out and sit in the next room for about ten minutes or so and go over all the things that we have discussed. Then, I will come back to give you some feedback on what I think might be helpful to you.

Another reason for using this technique is that it allows the worker to assess how closely she is "joining" with the client. There will be immediate feedback from the client on agreement or disagreement with the worker's input. A good joining with the client will produce what Milton Erickson calls "a yes set," nodding or some other indication that the client is in agreement with the worker. This can help to pace intervention with the client.

3. Normalizing

Most workers use this technique quite frequently and perhaps without having given a name to it. Sometimes it is called "universalizing." It is a technique of reassuring clients that what they are doing is within the range of normal human behavior, given their difficult circumstances. It is designed to reassure clients that their feelings, thoughts, and behavior do not mean that they are "mental," "crazy," or "off the wall," but fall quite within the normal range of human reactions.

Case Example

A young woman came to the attention of FBS because her four-year-old son "drove her crazy." The young mother's fiancé had died of Hodgkin's disease about three months prior to the contact. The couple had lived together for four years; the last two years had been very difficult as the man's illness became more serious and he required a great deal of care. The young woman also had an eight-month-old child from this relationship. The four-year-old son, from another relationship, became restless, more demanding, regressed to more infantile behaviors, and generally drove her "crazy." She said she saw signs of him being hyperactive with attention deficit disorder.

The young mother kept wondering what she was doing wrong, what she was doing that caused her son to misbehave. She kept complaining of her lack of energy, of feeling that she just couldn't get things done, and she found herself "losing it" with the child. She had slapped him too hard, which scared her, since this kind of behavior was out of character for her. The four-year-old had always been active, curious, and hard to control, but somehow she felt less effective with him in recent months.

The worker normalized her depression and her feeling of being overwhelmed. Many things were going on in her life at this time. She needed to grieve and mourn the loss of her lover; to adjust to being a single parent with two small children; to cope with a son who required an inordinate amount of structure and attention; and to cope with the pressure and complaints from her babysitter who threatened to quit because of the son's inability to follow directions.

The worker went a step further than just normalizing and told the client that it was actually amazing that things were not worse, given her very difficult circumstances. What she needed was to allow herself to grieve, give herself time to heal from the loss, and to gradually regain her previous level of competency.

Another way to normalize clients' concerns is to explain their problems as "stress" or reaction to "trauma." These are more hopeful, positive, and less damaging ways to help clients to view themselves. Everyone overcomes stress, and there are things clients can do to manage stress. Trauma implies that the difficulty is external to the client, and not caused by personal dysfunction, thus giving her hope that she can handle it and overcome it.

Case Example

Mr. and Mrs. P came to the attention of the FBS program when Mrs. P's 13-year-old daughter from her previous marriage got into a fistfight with her stepfather.

The couple's two-year marriage was full of conflicts over various issues such as how to discipline Mrs. P's two children; should Mr. P be the "authority" in the home; who should clean the house and do the dishes; how much free time Mrs. P should have as her own; what kind of food to buy and cook.

The couple fought frequently, accused each other of not caring, and of disrespect; at times they wondered if they were going to make it as a couple and a family. Had they done the right thing by getting married? Yet, both felt committed to making the marriage work since "down deep inside" they still cared about each other.

The team decided to see their problem from a developmental perspective and complimented the couple for "hanging in there" and trying to make the marriage work. The team told the couple, "We can easily see how overwhelming and hopeless it all seems to you at times. Well, no wonder. Most couples usually have some time to 'become a couple,' that is, time to work out the nitty-gritty of living with someone else in the same house, before they become parents. Just becoming a couple is itself hard work. Yet you started your marriage trying to learn to parent together while at the same time trying to learn to be a couple. No wonder you are so tired and feel overwhelmed and irritable at times. In your situation anybody would be." The team was, in fact, amazed that things were not worse than they were.

4. Illusion of Choice

People like to make choices, or at least want to believe that they are making choices. When working with FBS clients, presenting an illusion of choice can enable agreement. Through the experience of exercising choice, the client may accept an option that she might have found unpalatable otherwise. You can also teach parents to use this illusion of choice with their young children. It is known to work with adolescents as well as adults. Following are some examples of illusions of choice:

- Do you want to take your bath before you brush your teeth or after you brush your teeth?
- Do you want a medium helping of vegetables or a large helping of vegetables?
- Do you want to do your homework before you play or after you play?
- Would it be easier for you to have us visit you at 8 a.m. or at 11 a.m.?
- Do you want to work on your staying sober first or do you want to work on not getting depressed first?

As you can see from these examples, the important point of this approach is not the options themselves but the impression that the person has a choice. Small choices pave the way to bigger decisions by showing the decision-making process as a manageable one.

5. Reframing

Reframing is a gentle, yet potent way to help clients see their predicaments in a different light. This paves the way for them to find a different way to conceptualize the problem and helps to increase the possibility of finding new solutions to old problems.

Reframing is simply an alternate, usually a positive interpretation of troublesome behavior that gives a positive meaning to the client's interaction with those in her environment. It suggests a new and different way of behaving, freeing the client to alter behavior and making it possible to bring about changes while "saving face." As a result, the client sees her situation differently, and may even find solutions in ways that she did not expect.

You already have seen some examples of reframing in this book. For example, anger is labeled as intense caring, fighting can be a sign of one's independence, etc.

Following are some examples of reframing:

Lazy: laid back, mellow, relaxed, taking it easy
Pushy: assertive, in a hurry, action-oriented
Impatient: action-oriented, has high standards
Uncaring: detached, allows room for others
Depressed: overwhelmed, quiet, slowing down
Aggressive: forceful, unaware of his own strength
Nagging: concerned, trying to bring out the best in someone
Withdrawn: deep thinker, thoughtful, shy, quiet

Imagine yourself thinking about someone as "depressed." The way you behave toward someone who is "depressed" is quite different from your response to someone who is "overwhelmed, quiet, or slowed down." Helping the client reframe her own behavior will increase the possibility that she will think, feel, and act differently.

Use these steps when reframing a client's behavior or situation:

1. Think about what your current interpretation of the client's troublesome behavior.
2. Train yourself to think of a number of alternative interpretations of the same behavior.
3. Pick the one interpretation that seems most plausible and most fits the client's way of acting and thinking.

4. Formulate a sentence in your mind that describes the new positive interpretation.

5. Give the client feedback on what your thoughts are.

6. The client reaction will let you know whether your reframing fit her or not. A good fit will bring a visible change in the client. Some clients look stunned, shocked, amused; they may even start to laugh.

When you see any of these responses, you have found a good fit.

Case Example

Peggy, 32 years old, is a single parent of two daughters, Lisa, 14, and Melody, 11. She was referred to FBS by the intake worker following his investigation of alleged physical and psychological abuse of 14-year-old Lisa. Lisa reported that her mother kicks her, threatens to kill her, calls her "a slut, a whore" and so on. Lisa was in therapy for about six months, and her mother claimed that therapy made her "more uppity" and pulled her out of treatment.

Grandmother reported that Peggy is angry at the whole world and has alienated everyone in the family. At times, even grandmother is afraid of her.

It was easy to see why everyone labeled Peggy as angry, aggressive, and intimidating. She certainly came across that way to the worker. Peggy was clearly frustrated with Lisa's shoplifting, truancy, and excessive interest in boys.

Recognizing the importance of building a trusting relationship with Peggy if Lisa was going to be helped, the worker started by asking whether Peggy has always been so caring about Lisa. This was enough to bring tears to Peggy's eyes. She started to relate her special feelings for Lisa and thought that maybe she had spoiled Lisa by giving her everything she wanted. Peggy desperately wanted to protect Lisa from making the same mistakes she had made as a teenager.

In later contacts the worker reframed Peggy's tendency to jump into an argument with her family as her way of standing up for herself and doing what she believes is right, even when she pays a high price for it.

Parents' unreasonable expectations of children can be reframed as having high standards for them. A client's tendency to be "secretive" can be seen as her need for privacy, and, therefore, she should take all the time she needs to make sure that she feels safe enough to trust someone like the "welfare worker."

Case Example

Ron and Betty were married when they were 18 and 17, after Betty became pregnant. Life has not been easy for them; at times Ron held two jobs to keep things going when their three children were younger, and now they both have to work. During one of their intense arguments about Betty's tendency to be messy and Ron's frustration with it, Betty blurted out that Ron always had "common sense" when it came to decisions about the children; both agreed that Betty lacked in that area.

The worker immediately picked up on this and commented that "It may be true. But you certainly had enough sense to marry someone with common sense. What does that say about you?"

This little reframe changed the tone of the session from one of mutual blaming and criticism to one where they started to talk about how well they have done, given the difficult beginning they had.

6. *Keeping Track of What Goes Well*

"Between now and next time we see you, keep track of what goes well in your life that you want to see happen again and again."

In this directive, the attention is shifted to something someone is doing *well* and away from problems and failures. This task helps the client focus on what measures she takes to improve things and to notice the patterns of action and reaction in interpersonal relationships that are going well. This can give the client a feeling that she can successfully manage her life so that she gains a sense of control. Remember to phrase the task with "when," not "if." This implies that the client will overcome her urge to do undesirable things. Her attention is directed toward the positive things she does and not the times when things go badly.

7. *Externalizing the Problem*

This technique works well with children of all ages and with some adults. It is borrowed from the works of Michael White (1988, 1991), who started to use this approach to treat "temper" problems of children and adolescents. The strategy is to join forces with the client to "fight the devil" that causes the client to do things that get her into trouble.

This is a good strategy to use when it is not realistic to fight with the client or when she tends to put the blame on external things. The client can come up with various "monster taming" or "devil fighting" exercises to combat her problem behaviors.

Some alcohol or drug abuse treatment programs basically use the same principle when they teach abusers that the disease of the addiction takes over and controls them.

Clients, whether adolescents, adults, or children, can become enthusiastic about such things as building stamina; outsmarting the sneaky, devious, and cunning temptations of alcohol; and overcoming bad moods, laziness, a hot temper, the temptation to "flash," and other undesirable urges.

8. *Worker-Team (or Worker-Supervisor) Split*

This is a useful intervention when the client seems unable to decide between two equally compelling options or choices, for instance, choosing to take a chance on what the future might hold for her against deciding to put up with an unhappy, at times painful, but known and familiar relationship.

When the choice seem clear and obvious to the worker, it is easy and tempting to be lured into giving advice on what to do, only to be disappointed at the client's failure to follow through. A worker-team split is a good technique to get you out of this dilemma.

This simple technique is designed to highlight the client's ambivalence by having the worker side with the one side, while the team (or the invisible supervisor or team member) takes the opposite side of the ambivalence. This way, the worker heightens the difficulty of making the right decision while nonetheless framing the dilemma clearly and subtly helping the client weigh the options.

The following are two examples of difficult dilemmas that can force the worker to take sides.

A client is about to have his children taken away. In spite of his cocaine use, he has maintained a marginal level of parenting even though he slips now and then and exposes his children to potentially dangerous situations. Even though he gives lip service to wanting to keep the family together, he seems to be on the fence about how willing he is to work hard to keep the family together.

Or, a young mother was told that her 12-year-old daughter was sexually molested by her boyfriend. Medical examination and interviews with the 12-year-old were inconclusive. The client wants to be fair to her boyfriend and wants to believe her daughter, but doing both is difficult. Knowing what the consequences may be, she is extremely ambivalent and confused about what to do. She doesn't know whether she should leave the relationship or to stay. She can see the cost, benefit, and consequences of both choices.

How does the worker-team split work? The primary worker always takes the positive, healthy, motivated side that is willing to take risks in the search for solutions, while the team takes the other side, emphasizing the wish to keep things from changing.

At times the primary worker can take a "confused" stance while the team can split into two: "One half of the team thinks you should kick your boyfriend out, while the other half thinks you should keep him around, just in case he changes. I am not sure what is best for you since I can see that both sides have good points and bad points."

Case Example

Twenty-two-year-old Kathy, a mother of two, lives with her boyfriend, Ken, who abuses her. Although she feels angry and humiliated by his physical abuse, she makes excuses for his violence and for his alcohol and drug use. Her reasoning is that when he is not under the influence, he is loving, thoughtful, and a helpless "little boy" who needs her badly. She has been "in love" with him since she was 17, and she feels that because his family has rejected him he probably could not handle another rejection. Besides, she has "no place to go with two children." Ken says he is humiliated by being thrown out of the apartment by the police, and angered by Kathy's nagging, by her checking up on him everywhere he goes with his friends, and by her throwing things at him, pushing him, and shoving him.

Situations like Kathy and Ken's exasperate FBS workers everywhere. Frequently, the police and the district attorney's office become angry with such clients. Family members, friends, almost everyone becomes angry with the woman because when things go wrong, she is frantic to enlist their help and advice, but she never follows through when the crisis is over. Child care is neglected, the police are called, the boyfriend is evicted. The couple breaks up, and everyone breathes a sigh of relief, only to see them reconcile with promises to do better when, in fact, nothing has changed. Everyone is cautious, wondering when the cycle is going to start all over again. Most FBS workers are familiar with such cases.

Following one of Kathy and Ken's stormy fights, the team became very concerned and gave Kathy the following message during one of the sessions:

"Kathy, it is clear to all of us that you and Ken want to do what is good for all of you, and you both are having a difficult time doing it. The team is particularly concerned about the increasing violence between you and Ken and are very worried about both of your ability to protect yourself from harming each other and harming your children. The team wants you to give some serious thought to when you would say 'enough is enough': on your way to the hospital with a broken neck, or when one of you injures your children seriously, or on the way to the city morgue? On the other hand, I really don't know what to think about that since I know how much you want to do what is best for your children."

Kathy was visibly shaken by this, promised that she would not let the children be hurt, said she did not want to die, nor did she want to kill Ken. Kathy eventually left the relationship following another fight.

Workers without a team can still make use of this approach. The simplest way is to say to the client: "Half of me thinks this way, and the other half of me thinks that way, and frankly I am not sure which of the two is the better choice."

Another way to use the split to highlight the client's ambivalence is to say: "My many years of experience with your kind of problems would suggest you should go this way (specify one option), however, your problem is very unique and very different from most. Therefore, knowing your situation I might suggest that (the worker here suggests another option). I am not really sure what to suggest. I want you to think about all this and when we meet next time, tell me what steps you have taken."

9. *Keep Track of What You Do When You Overcome the Urge to . . .*

This message implies that good and positive things will happen in the client's life between sessions and the client is to watch for those positive things. This helps the client focus on what she does that helps her, and who does what to make things better.

For example, eight-year old Naco and ten-year old Nicolas were recently moved from a foster home to live with their grandmother when it was discovered that Naco was sexually abused in the foster home. Having lived alone for some time and now working at two jobs, the grandmother was at first reluctant to take the children but agreed, as their mother could not care for them because of her drug abuse.

The grandmother was quite defensive about her own child rearing practices and insisted that the mother was a good-hearted person who got sidetracked by drug use and the influence of bad people.

Deciding to accept her world view, for the time being at least, the workers initially gave the grandmother this task: "Keep track of what you notice happening with Naco and Nicolas that tells you that their living with you is good for them." Later on, the same task was phrased in more active terms: "We want you to keep track of what you do to help the children heal from the abuse."

If you have a client who sees herself as not having control of her life, this is a good way to get started. You may want to gradually change the sentence structure, for instance, from "could" and "would," to "will." Sometimes, these subtle changes are better, making it easier for the client to take credit for improvements she will be making.

10. Change a Small Element in a Familiar Pattern

This is the easiest, simplest task to give to the family. All patterns and sequences around problems and solutions are rule governed, and sometimes changing a small element of a pattern can make a big difference in the repetitive "same old problem."

For example, if the couple's fighting causes a problem for them and there is no exception to replicate, find out the details of the fighting pattern: where, how long, when, what about, who says what, what happens next, etc. Find out what is the smallest step they can change in the sequence and have them experiment with it. Changing the location of where they fight can make a big difference. They may agree to fight only in the bedroom, only outdoors, only about one topic at a time, never during a meal, or only while they are walking in the shopping mall (where there is the built in safety of being in a public place).

A parent who is frustrated with her teenage son not getting up for school on time, for example, tends to say the same thing: the same pleading, the same lecture, the same bargaining, the same threats, and the same punishments. When workers talk to the child, they will find that he can repeat word for word what his mother says to him. Children do listen to their parents but do not necessarily follow their directions. Not knowing this, most parents tend to repeat what they say until they are "blue in the face." Then they become frustrated because the child does not "listen."

A mother with this problem has a number of options, all related to her no longer doing "more of the same" but doing something different. She can stop reminding him about getting up for school; she can make him "work" at home. Since he refuses to "work" at school, he should "work" at home, such doing household chores, but he should not stay home and watch television. If the child's excuse is that he is too sick to go to school, even though there is no physical basis for it, he can be made to stay in bed all day, and not be allowed to get up, watch television, listen to music, etc. In other words, it should be more uncomfortable and inconvenient to be home than to be in school.

For couples whose fighting tend to get out of hand whenever they discuss touchy issues, they can make an arrangement with each other to discuss these only in public places, such as a coffee shop or over a sandwich at a restaurant. For some, but not all couples, this builds in protection against things getting out of hand. With clients who have work or job experience, the worker can suggest that every couple needs a business or staff meeting now and then and they should come to the meeting with a list of things to discuss. Some aspects of managing family life are a great deal like running a business.

With some couples, the worker can structure their "business" meetings by suggesting that the first meeting is only to list problems, a second meeting is to combine the two lists, the third meeting is to figure out possible solutions, and so on. This kind of step-by-step approach must be different enough from what they did before. Such differences, however small, increase the chances of success.

Case Example

Joe and Betty admitted that their disagreements about parenting frequently get out of hand. At times, both of their tempers flare up, and they end up hitting each other, especially if they are both under the influence of alcohol. They agreed that this not only is bad for their marriage but also is having a serious impact on their two children, who are beginning to mimic them by throwing things, calling each other bad names, and so on.

They report that they have never been able to work together as a team. Betty, who comes from a large family in which she raised many of her younger siblings, saw herself as an expert on child care, while Joe, who feels less sure of himself as a parent, was nevertheless eager to learn. Besides, he had some strong feelings about how a boy should be raised and wanted strong input into raising his sons.

The couple was told to do the following between sessions. They were to go to a public place, such as an inexpensive coffee shop. The goal for the first meeting was only to air their ideas on parenting, without trying to convince the other or trying to solve their differences. They were not to express their opinion about the other's views. When they finished expressing their views, they were free to do anything they wished, such as go to a movie, go for a drive, or whatever they agreed would be enjoyable.

During the second meeting, which was to occur within 48 hours of the first meeting, each was to offer an idea of what the compromise would look like and what action would be needed to implement the compromised view. They were only to air their opinions, and not to attempt to implement any of their ideas.

During the discussion of their fierce arguments, the worker realized that each was extremely sensitive to the other's subtle nonverbal cues, such as eyebrows being raised, even a slight shaking of the head, or closing of eyes, smirking when one disagreed, and so on. Whenever one of the partners noticed such subtle cues, he or she would become angry and then they would break into fierce fights. Recognizing this, the worker structured their discussion even further and recommended that they must sit side by side when they were to offer proposals for changes, again only in public places, and one step at a time. This was always followed by a pleasant time together.

When clients are offered and follow such step-by-step instructions that are tailored to their unique needs and situations, their safety is assured and they are likely to develop some solution-finding skills.

11. Secret Signs

Credit for this intervention goes to Charlie Johnson and Yvonne
Dolan, who told me about its effectiveness with violence-prone
families. This works well even when small children are involved.

Since safety is the most important factor when working with
families where violence has been a problem, this is worth a try.
As part of an understanding or a contract, the worker and all
family members have an agreement on a specific object (such as a
doll, a family treasure, a special toy, a souvenir item) that everyone will use as a signal. This item is located in a place that can be
easily reached by even a small child. Whenever anyone in the
family is afraid of violence or inappropriate touching, anyone in
the family is free to take the item. The disappearance of the item
is a signal to the rest of the family that someone in the family feels
unsafe and someone must call the worker or take other appropriate steps.

This kind of safety measure gives everyone in the family a sense
of control; it is something all family members can do to protect
themselves and the family, thus increasing the sense of safety,
which can lead to improved functioning and health.

12. Secret Comforting Note

This is another idea borrowed from my colleague Yvonne Dolan
that is helpful with an extremely damaged or traumatized client
or someone in a crisis. This intervention relies on and takes advantage of a person's innate self-healing capacity.

Have the client think of a word or a symbol of comforting
thoughts or a sentence that has a special meaning, such as a grandmother who was particularly nurturing but who is dead now; a
soothing or relaxing picture in one's mind; a phrase that has a
special positive meaning to the client. Have the client write that
word or phrase with her nondominant hand, and have her carry
that piece of paper with her wherever she goes. (When the client
uses the nondominant hand to write with, there is extra effort
required and the words may appear to be written in a childlike
way.) Whenever she becomes scared, insecure, or frightened, she

can take it out and be comforted. When the note is worn out or the meaning changes, the client can make another note.

13. Pretend That the Miracle Has Happened

When you get a good description of a miracle, pictured in a concrete, realistic, and measurable manner (see Chapter 7 for details on the miracle question), have the client pick a day when she is to "pretend that a miracle has happened and the problem that brought you to our attention is solved. Do everything you would do if the miracle happened, and keep track of what you notice that is different about yourself, your family, and how other people react to you."

Case Example

Fifteen-year-old Rex was a "pro" at therapy, having been through in-patient treatment several times and out-patient treatment (individual, group, and family counselling). He not only abused alcohol and drugs but also was a minor drug dealer. He was squeaking through school, with frequent truancy and failing grades even though he was very intelligent. His parents were constantly angry at him, felt worn out and were considering filing a Child in Need of Protective Service (CHIPS) petition as the final solution to their frustration.

When asked the miracle question during the assessment phase, Rex detailed all the things he would do: "I will get up at 6 o'clock on my own, eat a good breakfast, get to the bus on time, get to school, stay in school, pay attention, come home, do homework, talk with the family about the day during dinner, help clean up, maybe talk to friends on the phone, and go to bed." Listening to this, the mother burst out, "It's a miracle!" She was amazed at how much he knew what was expected of him.

The team decided to take advantage of Rex's tendency to be secretive by giving him the following intervention.

Rex was to pretend that the miracle happened one day and the problem that made his parents bring him to therapy was solved.

He was to choose one day each week during the next two weeks and do all the things he would do when the miracle happened. He was to keep it a secret from his parents which days he chose as his "miracle days," but was to pay attention to whether his parents noticed anything different about those days. The parents were to guess which day they thought that Rex was having his "miracle day" and to let him know which day they thought it was, not by discussing it but by giving him a small reward, such as a pat on the back, cooking his favorite food, or taking him for an ice cream.

Predictably, the parents were wrong in guessing which days they thought were "the miracle days" — they ended up with six days of miracles instead of the expected two.

14. Pink Elephant

This has been used successfully with children of all ages in all cultural settings. An adapted version of this intervention has been used with adults, also.

It is an ideal intervention for someone who feels helpless, powerless, or victimized in social relationships. Some children who are picked out as a target of bullies or teasing usually respond in a predictable manner; that is, they usually cower, look scared, or avoid eye contact with the other children who tease or bully them. As soon as the "bullies" approach them, the child usually runs away, bursts into tears, or tattles to the teacher or another adult. Such a reaction, in turn, brings on more teasing and bullying.

Workers can give these children a "secret weapon" when they appear ready to be a "customer."

"Jason, I want you to keep this a top secret. You cannot tell anyone about this, and this has to be kept an absolute secret for it to work. Whenever Jerry and his friends come near you and you think they are going to start teasing you, I want you to do three things. First, you imagine a huge pink elephant dropping from the sky and about to land on Jerry's head and squish him flat. Of course, you can see it but Jerry cannot. Second, every time you see him I want you to imagine that he has lost all his hair and all his teeth. So he is bald-headed and toothless. Third, I want you to imagine that his fly is open. Got it? When I see you next time I want you to tell me how things are different for you."

Case Example

A young woman was in tears as she described her encounters with her boss who "ranted and raved" at her. She liked her job very much and saw potential for moving up, but she was on the verge of quitting because of the intense conflict with her boss. The pattern she described was similar to Jason's: she would burst into tears, gets upset, and become less productive, which in turn invited her boss's wrath.

Since the pattern was similar to Jason's, it was decided to suggest to her a modified version of the "pink elephant" technique. It was suggested to the woman that the next time she has a run-in with her boss, she should pretend that her boss is stark naked when he yells and screams at her.

The following session she reported her discovery that her boss "ranted and raved" at everyone in the office. It was not her problem — he had poor interpersonal skills, and she decided not to take it personally. By focusing on her boss's irrational behavior instead of her own emotional reaction to what she believed was his unreasonable and unfair behavior she was able to see the boss for what he was. She decided to stay on the job.

Children like Jason, who feel victimized and powerless, need some secret weapon that will give them a sense of power and ability to control their lives. When Jason imagines revenge on the other child who picks on him, he is more likely to smile and act more confident and less likely to cower or run away. This interrupts their typical interaction patterns.

15. Prediction Task

At times clients report that exceptions to their problems do happen sometimes, but they see these exceptions as not within their control. They describe them as if they happen completely randomly and occur spontaneously. Since they cannot describe exactly how these exceptions occur, it is not reasonable to expect them to repeat those exceptions. The following task helps clients realize that those exceptions may be much more within their control than they thought.

A client is told to "make a prediction" each night about whether she will have a "good day" or a "bad day" the following day. The next day, she is to go about her usual routine. At the end of the day, she is to review the day and record whether it was a "good day" or a "bad day" and make another prediction for the following day. She is to repeat this until the next appointment.

Keeping a careful record of what the client predicted and how the day actually turned out will produce some interesting insights into the client's ability to make what appears to be a random or spontaneous exception into a deliberate one. My experience is that most clients predict many more "bad days" than they actually have. In the process of reviewing each day with the worker, the client discovers that her week turned out to be much better than she thought it would.

The worker can encourage and enhance the client's discovery of ways to "do more of" such deliberate exceptions, and thus, expand her own successes.

Case Example

Eleven-year-old Marcus was brought to the attention of the worker because of his long-standing problem of bedwetting. His foster mother was quite frustrated and tried everything she could to be helpful, but to no avail.

When the worker talked with Marcus alone, it was clear that he was embarrassed about the bedwetting and wanted to solve the problem. Various questions indicated that he was ready to be a "customer." He wanted to go to summer camp like other boys, sleep over at friends' houses, and so on, but he was reluctant to do so because of his problem.

Close questioning revealed that Marcus had many exceptions, such as when he slept over with his cousin at his grandma's house and at least once or twice a week in his own bed. Since he was unable to explain what the difference was between dry bed nights and wet bed nights, he saw these exceptions as random and completely out of his control. The team decided the prediction task would be appropriate.

He was given a daily chart on which he could make a prediction just before going to bed of whether or not he would have a dry bed. The following morning he was to record whether his prediction was correct or not. If his prediction proved wrong, he was to account for the incorrect prediction. If a correct prediction was made, he was to explain how he knew that. Either way he could be complimented for knowing what behavior was linked to his bedwetting.

In the meanwhile, the foster mother was told that Marcus was old enough to take care of changing the sheets, laundering them when necessary, and she was instructed to completely avoid checking his bed in the morning and scolding him about any wet beds. She was to also make a prediction of whether she thought Marcus would have a dry or wet bed each night and to keep track of the outcome. Both Marcus and the foster mother were to keep their prediction and the outcome a secret from each other and not to discuss them.

The following week Marcus proudly produced his record on the experiment. He had many more nights when his bed was dry. He explained that he cut down on drinking liquid and told himself he was going to have a dry bed. He added that he thought he was doing better in school and got along much better with his foster mother.

There are more complicated intervention techniques that can be borrowed from the family therapy field. But these 15 interventions listed are easy to follow and simple to do, and most clients of FBS respond quite well. As you can see, these intervention tasks are designed to elicit exceptions and to interrupt the patterns around problematic behaviors while relying on existing skills. The result is that they empower clients to discover and use their own resources. Along with the good interviewing skills described in Chapter 6, the techniques described here will be quite sufficient to begin to "do something different" with the majority of FBS cases.

10

Special Problems

THIS CHAPTER DESCRIBES some practical strategies and techniques that workers can use in their daily encounters to leave clients with feelings of hope for themselves. This chapter is not designed to be a comprehensive coverage of the various problem topics listed here. You are encouraged to study other more comprehensive literature on treatment issues for each individual topic.

LOOKING AT THE WHOLE FAMILY

It is easy to categorize a family as "a violence case," "an incest case," "an abuse case," or "a drug abuse case," and so on. This is a dangerous practice, because workers tend to concentrate on "the problem" and forget the people behind it. There is no single, typical picture of a violent family, incest family, or a drug or alcohol abuser. There are so many variations in family and problem configurations that such categories are almost meaningless in directing what the worker should be doing in the "trenches."

It is not helpful to rush in with a treatment plan that is imposed on the family. Individualized treatment, that is, treatment that makes sense to the client, seems reasonable from their world view, and is congruent with the way they do things, will increase cooperation, empower them, and will reduce worker frustration. Keep in mind that all families are different and, therefore, two families with the same drug abuse problem may require very different treatment approaches. A good posture to take is that even though you know a great deal about problems with families and human behavior in general and solutions to them, you are ignorant about this particular client's problems and his solutions.

Management of Crisis

Poor, "marginally functioning," ethnic minority, "borderline," or "multiproblem" families — and many other cases that come with descriptive or diagnostic labels — are thought to "thrive on crisis" and "live from crisis to crisis." It is sometimes believed that "crisis gives them some excitement in their dull lives." I believe such misconceptions about these families come from the fact that the client's contacts with the social services are typically sporadic and center around crises. Furthermore, workers tend to ignore these families' successful management of their lives between crises, noticing only the problems that trigger the crises.

A crisis can mean that something new is happening when the family is not ready for it or that something different needs to happen but is not happening. Crisis signals both a *danger* and an *opportunity*. That is, a crisis can be a signal that a problem could become worse if some change is not made, and it can also be an opportunity to bring about needed changes. Therefore, the worker's goal need not be limited to restoring the status quo but also to improving the functioning of the family unit.

The following are some guidelines for turning a crisis into an opportunity for growth:

1. *Find out what is different this time.* Why is the fight worse this time? (Clearly they fought many times before, so what is different about *this* fight?) Why is the client more upset about a loss of job, being laid off, the school calling, the child spilling milk, the wife leaving, the husband coming home "buzzed," so that events touched off a crisis this time?

Usually, what is different is not measured by the seriousness or the gravity of the "problem" itself but by the meaning or interpretation of the event to the person involved. He has been through the same thing many times before but somehow it means something different this time. Find out what that different meaning is to the client.

2. *What is the combination of event and reaction?* The trigger is hard to determine: What is the external reality that makes a crisis and the internal reaction to the external factors?

Case Example

Getting off welfare was important to Brenda and she was proud of finally finishing a job training program. She found a job that she thinks has a future potential for promotion with increased income and job security. However, during her probationary period on the job, she received many warnings about getting phone calls from school about her son Jimmy's behavior problems. Her supervisor believed not only that these frequent phone calls distracted her from concentrating on her work but also that the excessive request for absences in order to attend the school meetings interfered with her job performance.

In spite of the fact that they had many conversations during which she warned Jimmy about the danger of the loss of her job and what it would mean to the family's future, nothing seemed to help. One day Brenda went after Jimmy with a baseball bat when the school called her at her job and demanded that she come to pick him up because they had suspended him for three days. Fortunately Brenda was able to control herself just in time but she later requested service from FBS because it "scared the daylights out of" her. Her initial request was to place Jimmy out of the home in order to protect him because she had lost confidence in her ability to control herself.

The worker spent a great deal of time with Brenda talking about what was different about this last phone call, why she reacted so differently to Jimmy, and what she could have done to handle the crisis differently. Given Jimmy's tendency to be outspoken with teachers, his "class clown" behavior, and his not taking his studies seriously, Brenda agreed that she is likely to get another phone call from the school. She decided on steps that she can take next time not to jeopardize her job and not to "fly off the handle" were she to get another phone call from Jimmy's school.

Brenda recognized that in the past she tended to view Jimmy's misbehavior as something he was doing out of disrespect for her and out of lack of appreciation for how hard she was trying to keep the family together and off welfare. When Brenda further realized that Jimmy's problem maybe related to his own personality and he needed help in expressing himself differently in school she began to help him find avenues for more creative expression.

3. *Find out how the client has coped since the crisis.* Many clients and workers forget that most people somehow manage to deal with crisis on their own, even, if it is for a very short time. This "short time" between the phone call and your rushing to the scene may be only a half an hour or one day, but find out what the client did to cope during the period of waiting for help. Surprisingly, many clients find some way to cope with the difficulties on their own. Such coping skills and strategies need to be supported and pointed out so that the client can remember to do the same next time. This increases his sense of competency.

4. *How did the client handle past crisis successfully?* It is always helpful for the worker to find out how the client successfully handled a past crisis similar to this one. If the client has survived even worse crises than the current one, the worker needs to know what he did then and what aspect of that can be saved and applied here. Such transfer of learning is helpful to the client by conveying to him that we all learn from our successes and mistakes.

5. *"How come things are not worse?"* As you find out the details of the crisis, pay attention to what the client did right to contain the crisis and prevent it from getting worse. Clearly, you need to support and encourage him to "do more of" what worked this time and think of ways to repeat it next time.

Case Example

Fifteen-year-old Tara overdosed on her mother's tranquilizers and was passed out on the living room floor when her mother returned

from the laundromat. This was the first such episode. At first, the
mother thought Tara was catching up with her sleep, at worst,
maybe experimenting with drugs, and left her to sleep. Tara managed to signal to mother that she needed to go to the hospital, and
her mother responded promptly.

Later, when things had calmed down, the worker spent a considerable amount of time helping both Tara and mother figure
out how they both had done many things right in the crisis: how
Tara figured out that she needed to signal to her mother that she
needed help and how her mother had enough sense to listen to
Tara's attempt at communication. Tara's initiatives were praised
and credit was given to Tara for having enough trust in her
mother to let her know she needed help immediately. Credit was
also given to mother for getting Tara the medical attention she
needed.

Obviously, the reason for Tara's "cry for help" needed to be
addressed, but the early intervention in giving the client credit
built a positive relationship for subsequent work. Later Tara was
able to discuss with the worker about the intense peer pressure
and the fights she had in school, the threats of violence she received, her fear of "being jumped on," her troubles with teachers,
and so on.

6. *What have you learned about yourself (or your family) from
this crisis?* After the crisis is over, it is always useful for the worker
to help the client review the whole event. Each crisis can be
viewed as having taught us something new about ourselves. Thus,
asking the following questions not only will provide role modeling
but also will help the client to "save face."

- In looking back over the last couple of weeks, what do you
suppose you learned about yourself that you did not know before?
- Is that new for you? Did it surprise you?
- What would you say you did different this time than in the
past?
- What do you suppose your mother (or other significant person in the client's life) would say you learned from having gone
through what you have just been through?

7. *Not all crises are the same.* Remember that what is a crisis for one family is not necessarily a crisis for another, even if the incidents are identical. Each client's definition of crisis is very different, and their experience of the crisis is very different over time. For example, one person's experience of sexual abuse may be very different from another's. To treat them as if they were the same would be disrespectful of the particular person you are working with. Accept the client's definition as valid and relevant to him at this time.

I was once involved in a study of survival factors of breast cancer patients who outlived their physicians' prognoses. Part of the study involved asking patients about how they managed other crises in their lives in order to develop a list of skills that they could use in this present crisis. One 48-year-old woman reported that the most traumatic crisis she ever experienced in her life was when she was 22 years old. What could possibly be more traumatic than a diagnosis of cancer? She said her fiancé had jilted her, broken off their engagement, and married some other girl. Even though the woman knew that it would have been a disastrous marriage had she gone through with it, she explained that it was the most devastating experience she had ever had, even worse than the news that she had breast cancer.

The lesson here is that not all crises are the same for everyone.

8. *What is the first, early signal that a crisis is brewing?* Most clients can describe the early signs, "vibes," "hunches," or clues that "something is not going right." Workers need to spend some time discussing these early signs with families in detail. Questions to ask are:

a. What is the first clue to you that this argument is likely to become a fight?

b. What are steps you can take to keep the argument from getting out of hand?

c. What have you done successfully in the past that might work again?

d. How come other similar situation in recent times did not lead to crisis? Who did what, how, when differently so that you handled it? What have you learned from this?

e. What are the conditions or the triggers that are likely to lead to a crisis? Are you more likely to fight when you are tired? When you've been drinking? When the money runs out? When you've been under more stress?

When you have discussed these questions, you should be able to figure out what the steps the family needs to take to avoid another crisis. After a crisis, discuss with the family and find out what they learned from it. Such "debriefing" helps the family learn how to help themselves.

Case Example

This was the first marriage for Terry and the second for Gary; both agreed that it had been a "nightmare" since the wedding. Each had had considerable difficulties in previous relationships; Terry had been raped at 19, hospitalized after she went "psychotic" following the rape, and was on antipsychotic medication. She had joined a fundamental church, then had fallen out of it. She could only handle a third-shift job in a nursing home. Many attempts at relationships had not worked out for her. Gary's ex-wife had left him for another man. Some years ago he had cut off ties entirely with his adoptive mother. He was recovering from alcohol abuse but still "messed" with drugs now and then, and was a self-described "self-help group junkie." He flew into a rage whenever he saw Terry "primping herself" in public. He was "leaving the marriage" one day, then was in love with Terry the next.

Since the wedding, the couple had had a series of crises, which resulted in fighting that usually ended only when both were exhausted or hungry. One time the crisis ended in physical violence. Everything and anything—a disappointing holiday, a forgotten birthday, a phone call from Terry's mother, pictures of previous relationships—could trigger a chain-reaction pattern: one accused, the other defended and counter-accused, past grievances were listed, and there were frequent threats of leaving. They would end by making up, but the cycle was repeated almost every week. Gary was once taken to a hospital for an "anxiety attack" and Terry described herself as going "psychotic" during one of these fights.

A useful treatment strategy with the couple was to review and anticipate a potential crisis and debrief the past crisis during each contact. Each session was spent in thoroughly going over each item listed below:

a. There was a review of who did what, and how, to diffuse the crisis so that each episode did not end in violence.

b. Compliments were given to whomever had taken steps to not overact each time, however small or insignificant it seemed.

c. There was an examination of forthcoming events that might trigger either one to become upset.

d. Since any review of past events only triggered the blame, accusation, defending, counter-blaming pattern, the worker focused on successful strategies to avert *future* crises.

During one of the sessions Terry blurted out that she would get really upset if Gary forgot about Valentine's Day. It turned out that Gary had disappointed her on Christmas, Thanksgiving, her birthday, and many weekends, and that this usually ended in arguments. A large portion of the session was spent in reviewing past arguments and discussing what she might do differently next time so that there might be a chance of the situation ending differently. Terry decided to lower her expectations of Gary about such things. This was reframed as her way of learning to accept him because she loves him and her growing maturity in the relationship.

In the meantime Gary examined how he might do more small things for Terry such as bringing her a cup of coffee when she woke up, asking her how was her day, and finding ways to control his rage and jealousy. It was explained to Gary that he was learning to express his nurturing side and that he was learning to accept himself more fully.

MULTIPROBLEM FAMILIES

At times, some cases have so many problems and issues that even a seasoned worker can get overwhelmed and feel lost about where to begin. Many multiproblem cases can have one or more of the following components: chronic unemployment, frequent job changes, frequent address changes, chronic physical and mental illness, marital conflicts, truancy, delinquent behavior or poor academic performance of one or more children, long standing intergenerational conflicts, overinvolved extended families of origin, drug and alcohol abuse, sexual abuse of children, and so on.

Sometimes doing less accomplishes more and moving slowly gets you there faster. The common and immediate reaction to multiproblem families is to become overwhelmed and "bring out the cavalry" and parcel out the problems and treatment plans accordingly.

For example, each child is sent to a separate therapist. Someone is put on medication; day care for the children and job training for the adults are arranged. The family is bombarded with various programs out of a belief that "more and quicker is better." Not only is such a massive infusion of services confusing to clients, but also they cannot realistically manage all those schedules and appointments. In addition, it is difficult to know which of these services makes a difference or is effective. Such an approach has the effect of fragmenting the family. The clients are often given conflicting appointment schedules with professionals who offer different suggestions. Some treatment plans are made by the treatment providers without consulting the family or the other service providers. The result is unrealistic, unmanageable, and contradictory plans that the families cannot possibly follow through on. This frequently results in client noncompliance, premature termination, and in the family being labelled as "unmotivated" or "unreachable."

Since she is working with any number of combinations of problems, it is easy for the worker to move in and take over the solution-finding process. Remember the message that has been consistent throughout this book: The more clients solve their own problems, the more empowering it is to them and the more they become invested in their solutions.

The following are some guidelines you need to keep in mind as you proceed:

1. When confronted with a multiproblem family, do not panic; be calm and follow the following steps.

2. Ask the client what is the most urgent problem that he wants to solve first. Follow his direction, not yours. Be sure the goal is small, realistically achievable and simple.

3. Ask yourself who is most bothered by the problem. Make sure it is not you; you do not want to be the "customer" for your own services.

4. Get a good picture of how the client's life would change when that one goal is achieved. Find out how his life would be different then (see Chapter 8 for setting goals).

5. Stay focused on solving that one problem first. Do not let the fact that the client is overwhelmed affect you. Stay focused with the first goal until it is achieved.

6. Find out in detail how the client has made things better in the past. He needs to know what his own successful strategies are, which he can then apply to other problems.

7. Be sure to compliment the client on even the smallest progress and achievements. Always give the client the credit for successes.

8. When one problem is solved, review with the client how he solved it. What did he do that worked? How did he figure out to do it that way? In this new context of success, what does he need to do to solve the next problem? Remember that this is also a chance to empower him. In this way, multiproblem cases can be looked upon as multisolution cases, that is, there are numerous chances for finding solutions and successes.

VIOLENCE IN THE FAMILY

Psychological and physical violence in the family, whether between adults or between adult and child, is the most distressing kind of case that FBS workers encounter. In spite of many legal measures that exist in our society to handle such problems, it is always extremely stressful to workers to encounter any form of violence. Workers must be particularly alert to issues regarding personal safety.

Not All Violence Is the Same

Yet not all violence cases are the same. However, there is a rough pattern, and recent research information sheds new light on the causes and treatment of violence. What seems to be true is that some programs, such as PA (Parents Anonymous) groups, self-help groups, and education about the cycles of violence, are very helpful. But not all clients are able to make use of these groups or existing programs. Therefore, it is necessary to individualize treatment to fit the unique circumstances of the individual.

Management of violence is a very confusing issue because our society's response to violence is two pronged. One response is to deal with it by legal means, with punishment as the goal; the other approach is to see it as illness, with prevention and treatment as the goal. Whether the solution lies in social control or treatment is difficult to say, since there is no evidence that one is more successful than the other. Currently, both methods are used with limited success. Until we learn more about the best possible approach to control, treat, and prevent violence, we all must keep in mind the need for safety and improved functioning for the abused as well as the abuser.

Many studies indicate that forceful measures, such as calling the police, arresting the abuser, moving the abuser out of the home, or moving the abused to a shelter, are all useful to a point. Since most abusers are not likely to seek help on their own until they are forced to do so, these steps should be taken whenever warranted.

Those clients who are willing, with some encouragement, to use existing community resources, such as the shelter, self-help groups, and other training groups should be encouraged to do so. The majority of clients, however, are not likely to follow through on referrals to such resources when there is no legal mandate to do so. For them, the FBS worker may be the only person who can make impact on their pattern of violence.

Each case is unique, with special sets of problem configurations, resources, history and patterns of violence, motivation, and commitment to and investment in the relationship. Therefore, how you treat one violence case may be very different from how you treat another.

The more flexible your options and your approaches, the more likely you will be able to individualize your treatment strategies and, therefore, reach more clients. The more options you have about a case, the less likely you are to feel overwhelmed and stuck.

By the same token, clients also need to have many strategies and options that are available to them, such as either party leaving the scene, taking time out from arguments, being aware of what the trigger point is, discussing emotionally charged issues only in public places, making sure that weapons are taken out of the house, and learning to postpone emotionally charged decisions.

Case Example

Forty-three-year-old Tom was a Vietnam veteran with a long history of medical, psychiatric, and drug abuse problems. His second marriage, to Vicky, had been rocky and turbulent for the past eight years. During one of their many separations, Vicky had an affair. When he discovered this, Tom became abusive and threatened to shoot her with his gun, at which point Vicky left for a shelter.

Being unemployed, and perhaps unemployable, because of a back injury he sustained when he was a construction worker, Tom had taken over the homemaker's role, and Vicky went to work as a beautician. To earn extra cash, Vicky had customers come to the house in the evenings and weekends while Tom cooked, cleaned, and took care of their eight-year-old son and Vicky's 14-year-old daughter from a previous marriage. As Tom's depression increased, Vicky became increasingly resentful at having to support him financially with no hope in sight of change in their relationship.

Tom said that making the transition from the "macho" world of construction worker to that of homemaker had been very hard, and that he had been "going through hell" for the past two years of unemployment. His temper would flare up and he would become violent toward Vicky, especially when he felt unappreciated, nagged at, or felt demeaned because of having to ask for money from her. Both wanted to make their marriage work "for the children's sake."

It was found that discussions of emotionally charged issues, such as money, sex, Vicky's working long hours, Tom's poor house-keeping skills, and so on, often culminated in violence. During Vicky's stay at the shelter, they found that discussing these same issues on the phone was less likely to trigger intense and violent emotions. The couple agreed that whenever they needed to discuss trigger issues, they would do so only on the phone.

Case Example

Joe was a 29-year-old long-distance truck driver; his work schedule varied depending on where he was sent. He usually left home early Monday morning and frequently did not return until Friday night. Sometimes he would be "on the road" for two or three weeks. He was tearful when he called the hotline one Sunday morning asking for help with his violent temper. He related that he had "sent" his wife to the hospital on Friday night during one of those episodes in which he just "went off." When finally seen in an emergency session a couple of hours later, Joe was still shaken with remorse and shame. Even though his wife was invited to come to the session with Joe, she refused to come in because she was too embarrassed to show her injuries.

Joe related that he had been like a "walking time bomb" all his life. Since his youth he had been in many fights and could have easily killed someone with his violent temper. He recounted some hair-raising incidents in which he would go after several men alone and so scared the others that they would usually flee. He reported that his alcohol use did not seem to make any difference in the frequency and intensity of his temper, since he could be just as violent without drinking. He confessed, however, that his violence was most frequent at home. There had been times when he was shocked to find himself choking his wife. He had also knocked her to the ground, given her many bruises, and on several occasions had sent her to the hospital with broken bones. He would usually apologize profusely afterwards and promise never to do it again. This pattern was repeated almost monthly, although it did not always end in violence. Joe reported that he was critical of Sandy, yelled at her, and blamed her for minor frustrations at home.

Over the years, Sandy had been repeatedly advised by her family and friends to leave Joe. Once she called a shelter for battered women and arranged to get there with her two sons, but she changed her mind at the last moment. Instead, she went to look for Joe in a bar and brought him home.

So what was different this time, since she had been to the hospital before? She said that Joe had hit her on the left ear so badly that the doctor informed her that she could have lost her hearing permanently.

The therapist was curious about his more than ten years of truck driving without any incidents; Joe reported that he had earned a driver safety award, so the worker asked how he managed not to lose his temper on the road. Highway driving, for days and weeks on end, encountering all types of drivers and situations, would be a very stressful situation for most people. Joe, in a matter of fact manner, related that he couldn't afford to fool around on his job. He said that he never drank alcohol or used drugs while on the road. "The strongest stuff I drink is coffee," he said proudly. He added that even though he becomes irritated with his supervisor, who makes unrealistic demands on his driving schedules, Joe never lost his temper. In fact, he proudly related that when he had quit the company a year before, his boss had asked him to return, offering him a pay increase. However, whenever he would get on the CB radio with Sandy, which is how he keeps in touch with his family, he would often "blow a fuse," be critical of her, and lose his temper. He thought that she deserved to be "treated as a lady" and listed many reasons for this.

Viewing this "on the road" behavior as an exception to his problems, the worker kept pursuing how he managed his "on the job" behaviors and how he "kept his cool" with other drivers on the road. He was surprised to find himself answering, "I don't dare lose my temper on the job because I could lose my job." He said he needed the job to support his family financially and he was proud of having done so for the past eight years. While on the job, he maintained a sense of humor and had perfect control over his emotions and behaviors. Surprisingly, he had never lost his temper with his two children (aged four and six) and had never abused them. In fact, Sandy criticized him for being too lenient with them. He thought his children were "funny," loved to wrestle with them, played with them, and was generous with affection and love. Use of the scaling questions indicated that he was highly motivated to keep the family together.

At the end of the session, after the intrasession consultation with the team, the worker gave the following feedback to Joe:

1. He was complimented for recognizing the problem and taking steps, such as calling the hotline, coming in for a session on a Sunday, and admitting that he has a problem.

2. He was complimented for taking responsibility for his violence, for not blaming his wife or external events, and for recognizing that she deserved to be treated as a lady.

3. He was complimented for taking his job seriously and for having learned what he needs to do to be good at it. Clearly he loved his family very much, since he was a hard worker and wanted to be a good husband and father.

4. It would not be an easy task to turn around his lifelong problem of a violent temper. But since he had already learned how to do a good job of it at work, his next task was to learn to do a better job at home.

5. Since he was scheduled to be "on the road" for three weeks before returning home, it would be a good opportunity for him to learn more about his "on the job" behaviors. Therefore, he was asked to keep track of these behaviors and see how he was doing a better job as a husband while he talked to Sandy on the radio.

During a session a week later, Sandy reported her decision not to leave Joe since she loved him very much. Her most recent medical checkup had revealed that, she would not lose her hearing. She was informed about her legal right to protection but insisted that she would never report Joe to the police, since he was a good father and a good provider, and she really had every intention of keeping the family together. She was hopeful, since this was the first time Joe had sought help on his own.

Subsequent follow-up contacts revealed that Joe was doing remarkably well. At the six-month follow-up they reported that there had not been a single episode of violence. Sandy was continually amazed at Joe's ability to "just walk away" from confrontations, which in the past would have triggered him to explode.

Reminder for the Worker

Since violence — physical, sexual, or verbal — tends to evoke strong emotional reactions on the part of workers, it is crucial that FBS workers seek help from peers, supervisors, or consultants in order to maintain their neutrality and not take sides with family members. The most difficult and yet important things to remember in treating cases where there is repeated violence are:

1. to not side with the victim against the perpetrator
2. to refrain from making and forcing decisions on the victim to leave the relationship.

Remember, the victim's family, friends, neighbors, and previous workers all gave the same advice. Since he did not follow their suggestions, you do not want to repeat what didn't work. A better way to handle the situation is to gently repeat questions such as, "What will make you say to yourself and to your boyfriend, 'Enough is enough?'" or "What does your girlfriend have to do before you will say 'this is enough; I deserve better than this?'"

Sexual Abuse

It has been estimated that at least one in four girls and one in eight boys are sexually molested before reaching adulthood. The perpetrator in the majority of cases is a family member or a close friend of the family. Clearly, it is a family problem and many studies document that family treatment is the most effective approach for both adult and sibling sexual abuse.

Sexual abuse is traumatic, devastating, and degrading to a child and can leave a profound psychological mark. The child protection services and FBS workers should be trained to provide the most updated, effective treatment approaches that will maximize the healing process. Since the FBS workers enter into the family system after abuse has been discovered, the primary task is to protect the child from further abuse. After this, then the healing process for the child and family can be started. A combination of punishment and treatment can be effective. Treatment should be focused on empowering the child and on putting the nonabusing parent or some other capable adult in charge of safety and protection of the child. Since there are many complex legal and treatment issues related to any sexual abuse case, this calls for specialized treatment approaches with a view toward safety, prevention, empowering the child, and preserving family ties.

Before a referral to another agency is made, the following questions should be considered:

1. Is the adult in this family able to follow through on the referral?
2. Will individual treatment further fragment the family, which is already suffering from intergenerational boundary violations?
3. What is the first task for the family?
4. What are the worker's criteria for safety for the child?
5. Do the existing resources in the community meet the family's needs right now? Will they in the future?
6. What can the worker do to make sure that the "cure is not worse than the disease?"

Workers need to be familiar with the current policies on handling both adult sexual abuse cases and sibling sexual abuse cases.

What to Do When There Has Been Abuse While in Treatment

The roles of social control agent and treatment provider (healing, soothing, nurturing) often seem to clash and conflict with each other. The constant juggling involved in fulfilling these two roles is confusing to the worker and the client alike. Yet the worker's role is not only to investigate mistakes but also to strengthen family relationships, so that the client can move forward with his life. Gauging what is the most ethical, responsible, and legal way to behave as a professional is not a simple matter. Each case we work with calls for a continuous balancing act between what is legally and ethically responsible. For each situation, we must continually struggle to maintain this balance; there is no simple formula to rely on.

One option is for the primary worker to remain treatment oriented and be the "good cop," while the secondary worker can be the "bad cop" who enforces the control element of the law. Ideally, both the social control and treatment roles stem from the same goal: to strengthen the emotional bond of the family unit, thus building a foundation for stability and health. Whether one takes an investigative or a treatment role, both activities go on continuously throughout contact with a family. I contend that it is possible to do an investigation in a therapeutic manner and that treatment can also be investigative. There is no either/or split between the two.

When working without a team, a frank and open discussion of the worker's dilemma with the client is very helpful. Even when recommending the removal of a child from the home, if the worker does so with respect for the dignity of the client, my experience is that the client will be receptive to working with the worker again in the future. It is better for the worker to assume that most clients know right from wrong. Once again, it is important for the worker to keep in mind that each client and each case is different. All sexual abuse cases are not the same. Therefore, treatment needs to be individually tailored to fit the situation.

ALCOHOL AND DRUG ABUSE

It is estimated that somewhere between 50 and 80% of FBS cases involve drug and alcohol abuse. Therefore, each FBS worker must be able to assess how a client's drug and alcohol abuse is interfering with their ability to function as a parent.

There are many claims and counterclaims about the most effective, efficient, and successful treatment methods for drug and alcohol abuse. While we are waiting for conclusive data from research that will tell us what might be the best treatment method for different kinds of clients, the available research suggests that an individualized treatment approach works best. The exhaustive study by the Institute of Medicine (1990) strongly advocates preventive measures, early intervention, an individualized approach, and recognition of the validity and value of nontraditional treatment.

Most experts in the field agree that the success rate—when success is defined as total abstinence—in alcohol treatment is poor—approximately 10% of patients maintain long-term sobriety (defined as four years or longer) (Gottheil et al., 1982; Helzer, Robins, Taylor et al., 1985). On the other hand, it is generally accepted that most treatment has the positive outcome of a reduction in alcohol consumption and an improvement in quality of life for two-thirds of those who undergo treatment. Therefore, the question is whether the treatment methods are unsuccessful or whether the criteria for success should be revised. Many advocate (Miller, 1985) that total abstinence should not be the sole criteria for successful outcome. Much research and clinical experience indicates that the client motivation for treatment is directly related to the treatment success.

FBS workers cannot ignore the cost of treatment involved because of the economic realities of the client population. Much of the research data indicate that there is no appreciable difference in the outcome between short-term and the traditional long-term treatment, inpatient or outpatient treatment of alcohol abuse (Fingarette, 1988; Hester & Miller, 1989; Holden, 1986, 1987).

Many inpatient treatment programs for drug and alcohol abuse are moving toward a shorter period of stay in treatment facilities because of rising costs. For many clients, especially those who participate in Health Maintenance Organizations, the inpatient stay becomes shorter and shorter, from 14 days to 10 days, even to in-home detoxification. The traditional 28 days of treatment is no longer the rule. Most common is three to seven days of inpatient detoxification under medical supervision, followed by day-treatment programs and outpatient treatment, self-help programs such as the Serenity Club, AA, Al-Anon, and the sponsor system.

Most social service programs recognize the serious nature of substance abuse and its devastating effect on families. They offer a variety of services designed to minimize such effects. Most FBS programs have access to such services. Coordination of services and cooperation of the FBS workers and special services are crucial to success.

As most treatment programs have high relapse rates, the emphasis should be on changing the client's environment so that it is conducive to maintaining the treatment goal when he returns from the program. Clients who return to the same family and social network, to the same abusing environment and life styles, are high risks for relapse. Many studies conclude that the success rate is higher when the abuser has family support or a meaningful job, as these give strong motivation for treatment. In other words, when the client has more to lose he tends to be more motivated.

Since most of the existing treatment models must rely on voluntary participation, acknowledgement of problems, and acceptance of treatment to be successful, FBS workers might be the only professional person who has access to those clients who will not avail themselves of treatment programs. Therefore, it is crucial that the workers in the FBS program have knowledge of and familiarity with substance abuse problems so that they can make use of the opportunities that their contacts with such clients offer.

The following are some helpful suggestions for workers. Clearly, not all clients will respond the same way; therefore, it is important for the worker to individualize the approaches used for each client. (For a more comprehensive, detailed treatment approach, see Berg & Miller, 1992.)

Management of Denial

Denial of substance use is very common in encounters with clients who show many telltale signs of substance abuse, such as not paying the rent, having no food in the house, accumulating utility bills, and so on. Instead of trying to be subtle about your suspicion of drug or alcohol abuse, a straightforward question, asked in the most matter-of-fact manner, about their daily use can be effective. This must occur after a fair amount of "joining" with the client is done and a good working relationship is established. The following approach maybe useful when approaching the subject for the first time.

> I can see that your life is very stressful. You have many serious problems to put up with. And I know that many people in your situation use drugs or drinking to cope with life's difficulties. What do you do that helps you from using too much drugs or alcohol?

The usual confrontation of substance use has limited success because if such action does not produce the desired result, the next logical step is to allow the client to "hit bottom." It is my contention that such a drastic move should be used only in limited situations as a last resort, *not* as the first step. The above approach normalizes the drug and alcohol use but lets the client know that he has serious problems with which it is difficult to cope. The worker assumes that the client uses drugs or alcohol, but the question is how much or how little is used. Drug use is handled as if it is the reasonable thing to do under the circumstances, making the client feel less defensive in talking about it. The following is a common response.

> Client: Well, I try to use only a little. I don't use it much. I know I shouldn't, but my friends give me some.

> Worker: So, what do you have to do so that you do what is good for you and your children?

Obviously, not all clients respond this way. When they are still skeptical of the worker's motives and deny the problem, the worker still has several options.

Worker-team split. The primary worker takes the client's side while the secondary worker or someone else, such as the supervisor, confronts the client.

> As you know, I have been discussing your situation with my supervisor (or a team). She is convinced that there is drug abuse involved here and insists that I am being fooled by you. But I

know you are not that kind of person because you have been pretty straight with me. So I don't know what to think. What do you think?

This "confusion technique" puts a lot of pressure on the client, perhaps even more than a direct confrontation. Many clients have been repeatedly told that they should do something about their substance abuse and are very skillful at putting off those caring and concerned family members and friends.

As I get to know you, I have a fairly good idea about how difficult your life is. I also have a fairly long experience in working with people who use drugs and alcohol. I am confused. Everything about your situation says that you must be using drugs but you are saying you are not using drugs. It just doesn't add up. Maybe you can help me out.

When these methods do not work, you can always use the confrontation of problems or a urine test. Some clients will respond better to legal, or forceful and demanding approaches. The risk is that you may lose the contact with the client or he may adopt a passive-aggressive way to deal with your forceful approaches. Prochaska, DiClemente, and Norcross (1992) have written a great deal about the need to match the treatment to the client's readiness to change in order for the treatment to be successful.

Client involvement in setting goals. Many studies indicate (Miller, 1985) that when clients participate in setting goals, whatever the problem and particularly with alcohol abuse, the success rate improves.

Since the FBS program's goal is to preserve the family unit while insuring the safety of the children, the worker must always be clear about how the client's drug use enters into and interferes with his ability to keep the family together and how it affects the safety of the children.

In the beginning, the client may decide on a sporadic use of drugs and/or alcohol and may be reluctant to commit to total abstinence. Although not ideal, it is a worthy goal to pursue, because if the client can demonstrate that he can manage his use to a small degree to start with, then he can be helped to increase the period of nonuse. It is a small start. If the client cannot maintain his initial goal of limiting his use of alcohol or abstaining for a 30-day trial period, then the client must face reality. When given such a choice, many studies indicate that clients tend to choose more restrictive treatment options rather than less.

Relapses

Ideally when a client completes a treatment program, he will maintain complete abstinence. However, in reality, both worker and client can expect occasional setbacks. Expecting and making plans to manage relapses is not the same as encouraging them. It is prudent and realistic to equip clients with ways to prevent, manage, and control relapse, to recover, and to "get back on the right track" as soon as possible.

For most abusers and drug-dependent persons, to stop using is not hard. They do it every week. *Staying* clean is the harder task to accomplish. The maintenance of sobriety is often more difficult to do than "jumping on the wagon." My clinical experience suggests that what the worker does to focus on maintaining sobriety is different from activities directed at prevention of relapse. Membership in AA, NA, CA, or other self-help groups is a good way to maintain sobriety and learn a new life style, which is a difficult task in itself requiring strong support and commitment.

Since most experts in the field of alcohol treatment contend that one or two relapses a year is considered normal, what should the worker do? The greatest hazard of relapse is the client's own sense of failure and shame at his "weakness" and lack of strong will to live up to his promise to himself and to others. This can be quite discouraging for clients and they often feel that "having to start all over" is hopeless and futile. Indeed, such a view can be overwhelming. Clients need help in recognizing that a relapse does not mean that they must start over but that it is a small setback from which they know how to return quickly to the previous level of success.

Frequently, a detailed analysis, with the emphasis on future steps rather than past failures, will point out what the client needs to do differently next time and what strategies he must develop to manage his vulnerable point.

How Come Things Are Not Worse?

Instead of looking at relapse as a failure, workers can reframe the relapse as the client's internal reminder that he is still a "recovering person" and that he needs to be more vigilant about his recovery process. The following steps constitute a helpful checklist for the worker to follow when the client reports a relapse:

1. Find out what about this relapse is different from the last time. Any small but significant differences should be noted so that the client can see that he is making progress.
2. Ask how the client managed to stop at the point where he stopped. How did he know to stop at five drinks and not go further? What did he do to stop himself there? What internal or external cues did he respond to?
3. What did he learn from this episode that he can apply to the next situation?
4. Find out what the client does between relapses that is good for him and what he needs to "do more of." They may be such things as keeping busy, exercising, eating healthy, being productive, etc.
5. Get the client to anticipate the danger points, such as birthdays, parties, outings, holidays, that were occasions for abusing. Devise realistic strategies for nonuse.
6. Continue to pay attention to life-style changes or change of friends, social groups, and contacts.
7. Pay attention to the client's larger system issues and watch for "ripple effects."
8. Continue to support the client through compliments and cheerleading.
9. Reframe the relapse as his unconscious way of reminding himself that he is still an abuser and that he still needs to take "one day at a time."

THOSE "GOD-AWFUL" CASES

Thankfully all workers do not have to mumble these words under their breath too often, but most have said them from time to time. It seems that nothing you do seems to help, and you have tried everything you can think of. Even "miracle questions" do not seem to help.

What to do if you have one of these cases.

1. Relax. You are not alone. Everybody has these cases.

2. Review to check if you have a "customer." The "customer" may not necessarily be the client. Perhaps it is the court, the school, a disgruntled relative, your supervisor, or even you. Review Chapter 2 for further information.

Case Example

The court ordered that Marcus, aged 14, had to be in school, get a job, keep curfew, enroll in a drug treatment program, stay out of trouble with the police, and receive family counseling from the FBS.

The worker discovered that Marcus had had a series of difficulties with the court and the school. He is a gang member, and most of his friends were in the juvenile corrections facility; serving time at such a facility was a badge of honor and a guarantee of admission to the gang. He had not been in school for the past two years. His mother was chronically mentally ill, his father was in jail, there had been no contact with the family, and there were no relatives who could effectively take control of the family or of Marcus. It was not difficult for the worker to see that Marcus's 12-year-old brother was already out of control.

The worker also found that Marcus dealt drugs, and his income supplemented the AFDC (Aid to Families with Dependent Children) his mother received. It was clear that the mother depended on Marcus to supplement this income so that she could buy extra things for the children. Therefore, she was in no position to insist that Marcus stay in school or keep the curfew. Marcus told his mother off at times about her poor parenting. Because she knew that she was dependent on Marcus, the mother was cautious and would not discuss her concerns about his future. She was afraid of life without Marcus.

Clearly, this was more than a family problem. It was a massive social problem that FBS could not solve. The "customer" here was the community, yet the community was not ready to take action. With such cases, the worker needs to sort out repeatedly who is the "customer" for which problem.

3. *Review to check that you have a customer for change.* With some cases, your job may be to maintain a status quo and not necessarily to make any changes. With these cases your goal may be to act as a case manager, with the emphasis on maintenance, not change.

4. *Review to check you have the right goal.* Are you working toward the same goal as the client? Does the client really want to change or are they saying so because they are trained to say the right words? Clients may need help in sorting out realistic goals for their circumstances. Be realistic.

5. *Check to see if you have already achieved the goal without knowing it.* Review your initial assessment notes to see if you and the client have already achieved the initial goal without being aware of it. You may not have given yourself and the client enough credit for a small success.

6. *Make sure that consultation and supervision is available to you.* The availability of formal or peer supervision/consultation on an ongoing basis is essential to you. Have brainstorming sessions with your colleagues on those "god-awful" cases and get someone else's opinion. Sometimes, it is reassuring to know that your colleagues or supervisors find these cases just as "awful" as you do.

A supportive atmosphere for workers is crucial. There needs to be regularly scheduled staff meetings about cases so that helpful techniques can be shared. A certain amount of griping about clients or venting frustration about the system can be helpful at times, but such discussions should not be allowed to turn into regular "bitching sessions." Positive, constructive ideas should emerge from such meetings.

7. *Learn from successes and mistakes.* Each family offers us a rich learning experience, and we need to be grateful to them for

making us feel successful as well as keeping us humble. Analyze your successes as well as mistakes. The common tendency is to focus on failures and mistakes. It is important to know the mistakes, but it is also crucial that workers look at what they did right. Keep these successes in mind and apply them to other cases.

8. *Remember that you are making a difference in the client's life.* Always remember that you are making a positive difference with every exchange of words, meeting, or contact you have with your client. You are making an important difference in someone's life. This is the best reward for doing what you are doing. Your professional commitment to helping those who are the most vulnerable, helpless, and in need of help is remarkable. Keep doing all the good things you are doing.

Postscript

SINCE THIS BOOK WAS FIRST written I have become familiar with many more home-based programs across the U.S. and Canada as a trainer, program consultant, and supervisor. Along the way I have interviewed many families who were participating and benefiting from their involvement in the FBS programs. These opportunities to touch and learn from the lives of families and their workers everywhere inspire my faith about the innate goodness and the drive toward health in all of us. It also reminds me how we need to have hope about ourselves and about each other. I met hundreds of workers who keep this hope alive in their clients and in themselves in spite of the impossible barriers and adversities they face each day.

A colleague who has been in the child welfare system in Oregon for many years typifies many of the FBS workers I met. He says that despite the feelings he frequently gets from his work that the child welfare system "chews up the workers and spits them out," he loves the work and will never leave the field. It reminds me of why I stay in this field and what keeps me going when I feel like I can't take one more day of watching the suffering and pain in this world. What keeps me going is what I can only call blind faith, since there is no empirical data to support my belief. My faith is that *all* clients possess the resources to solve their problems; all clients know what is best for them; and all clients are doing the best they can right now under very difficult circumstances. I cannot expect anything more of anyone, including myself, but that we do the best we can right now and hope for the best in the future.

The small differences we make in our clients' lives touch our own lives in countless ways. While we are helping families, they in turn help us to learn about ourselves and to grow as a result. I cannot think of any other field I would want to be in; I feel privileged to be doing this work and I hope I have contributed a little bit toward making your everyday work a little bit more of dignity and respect. This in turn will make it possible for them to be a little more gentle and respectful of their children. What more can anyone ask for?

References

Berg, I. K. (1988). Marital therapy with one spouse or both. In E. Nunnally, K. Chilman, & E. Cox (Eds.), *Families in trouble* (vol. 3). Newbury Park, CA: Sage.

Berg, I. K. (1988a). Brief treatment of a homeless alcoholic: A case. In T. Todd & M. Selekman (Eds.), *Family therapy approaches with adolescent substance abusers*. Boston: Allyn & Bacon.

Berg, I. K., & Hopwood, L. (1991). Doing with very little: Treatment of homeless substance abusers. *Journal of Independent Social Work, 5*, 109–119.

Berg, I. K., & Miller, S. (1992). *Working with the problem drinker*. New York: W. W. Norton.

Boyd-Franklin, N. (1989). *Black families in therapy: A multisystems approach*. New York: Guilford.

de Shazer, S. (1982). *Patterns of brief family therapy: An ecosystemic approach*. New York: Guilford.

de Shazer, S. (1985). *Keys to solution in brief therapy*. New York: W. W. Norton.

de Shazer, S. (1988). *Clues: Investigating solutions in brief therapy*. New York: W. W. Norton.

de Shazer, S. (1991). *Putting difference to work*. New York: W. W. Norton.

Dolan, Y. (1991). *Resolving sexual abuse*. New York: W. W. Norton.

Edna McConnell Clark Foundation. (1985). *Keeping families together: The case for family preservation*. New York: Author.

Fingarette, H. (1988). *Heavy drinking: The myth of alcoholism as a disease*. Berkeley: University of California Press.

Furman, B., & Ahola, T. (1992). *Solution talk*. New York: W. W. Norton.

Gottheil, E., et al. (1982). Follow-up of abstinent and nonabstinent alcoholics. *American Journal of Psychiatry, 139*, 564.

Helzer, J. E., Robins, L. N., Taylor, J. R., et al. (1985). The context of long-term drinking among alcoholics discharged from medical and psychiatric facilities. *New England Journal of Medicine, 312,* 1678–1682.

Hester, R., & Miller, W. (1989). *Handbook of alcoholism treatment approaches: An effective alternative.* Elmsford, NY: Pergamon Press.

Holden, C. (1986). Alcohol consumption down, research up (letter). *Science, 198,* 773.

Holden, C. (1987). Is alcoholism treatment effective? *Science, 236,* 20–22.

Institute of Medicine. (1990). *Broadening the base of treatment for alcohol problems.* Washington, DC: US Government Printing Office.

Kiser, D. (1988). An unpublished follow-up study conducted at Brief Family Therapy Center, Milwaukee, WI.

Kral, R. (1987). *Strategies that work: Techniques for solution in the schools.* Milwaukee, WI: Brief Family Therapy Center Press.

Lum, D. (1992). *Social work practice and people of color: A process-stage approach* (2nd ed.). Pacific Grove, CA: Brooks/Cole.

Malan, D. (1976). *The frontier of brief psychotherapy.* New York: Plenum.

Mann, J. (1973). *Time-limited psychotherapy.* Cambridge, MA: Harvard University Press.

Miller, W. (1985). Motivation for treatment: A review with special emphasis on alcoholism. *Psychological Bulletin, 98*(1), 84–107.

Prochaska, J., DiClemente, C., & Norcross, J. (1992). In search of how people change: Application to addictive behaviors. *American Psychologist, 47*(9), 1102–1114.

Saleebey, D. (Ed.). (1992). *The strengths perspective in social work practice.* New York: Longman.

Sifneos, P. (1965). Seven years' experience with short-term dynamic psychotherapy. 6th International Congress of Psychotherapy.

Sifneos, P. (1985). Short-term dynamic psychotherapy of phobic and mildly obsessive-compulsive patients. *American Journal of Psychotherapy, 39*(3), 314–322.

Stone, E. (1988). *Black sheep and kissing cousins: How our family stories shape us.* New York: Penguin.

Stroul, B. (1988). *Series on community-based services for children and adolescents who are severely emotionally disturbed. Vol. 1: Home-based services.* Washington, DC: Georgetown University Child Development Center, CASSP Technical Assistance Center.

Walter, J., & Peller, J. (1992). *Becoming solution-focused in brief therapy.* New York: Brunner/Mazel.

Watzlawick, P., Weakland, J., & Fisch, R. (1974). *Change: Principles of problem formation and problem resolution.* New York: W. W. Norton.

Weiner-Davis, M., de Shazer, S., & Gingerich, W. (1987). Building on pre-treatment change to construct the therapeutic solution: An exploratory study. *Journal of Marital and Family Therapy, 13*(4), 359–365.

White, M. (1988). The externalizing of the problem. *Dulwich Centre Review.*

White, M. (1991). Deconstruction and therapy. *Dulwich Centre Newsletter.*

Index